What people are saying about

Walks with Sam

Thoroughly delightful. David W. Berner describes his beloved dog Sam as "a teacher of the perfect way to move in the world." And with that, Berner embarks on a season of dog walks, mindfully following Sam's lead in opening himself more fully to the thoughts, perceptions, and encounters that cross their path. Effortlessly runs the gamut from the profundity of Berner's musing on mortality, to the surprises that lurk within the seemingly mundane. A lovely testimony to the ways in which intention transforms our experience of our own lives.
Barbara Monier, author of *Pushing the River*

As Kierkegaard once wisely said, "If you just keep walking, everything will be all right." On a sabbatical from teaching, author David W. Berner begins a series of daily walks with his dog Sam. What from outward appearance to others would appear to be a regular jaunt to exercise a beloved pet is inwardly a reflective journey as the world is explored by both two and four-legged friend. Each walk takes its tone from the lay of the land, from the people and dogs they meet, from the signs of a society that has forgotten how to slow down in wonder and empathy.

With gentle humor and brilliant musings, both past and present, *Walks with Sam* has the charm and the innate truthfulness that some find in a wor̶ ̶h wonder and mystery with each  ̶e Book of
L.B. Johnson, Amazor
Barkley – Love and Life 1 ̶triever

An element that is a constant in David's writing is his enormous sense of humanity. He is as much a philosopher of the porch swing variety as anyone writing today.

San Francisco Review of Books

This is a sweet book from a sincere, thoughtful soul. As Thoreau found the whole world in his saunterings around Concord, Berner finds it walking his beloved dog Sam in an ordinary suburban neighborhood. His musings have a lovely, quiet inwardness, as he contemplates youth and age, continuity and change, community and solitude, love and envy, mourning and celebration — all with the subtle guidance of the dog he calls "the most mindful monk I know, a teacher of the perfect way to move in the world."

Dean Sluyter, author of *Natural Meditation* and *Fear Less*

Walks with Sam

A man, a dog, and a season of awakening

Walks with Sam

A man, a dog, and a season of awakening

David W. Berner

ROUNDFIRE
BOOKS

Winchester, UK
Washington, USA

First published by Roundfire Books, 2020
Roundfire Books is an imprint of John Hunt Publishing Ltd., No. 3 East St., Alresford,
Hampshire SO24 9EE, UK
office@jhpbooks.com
www.johnhuntpublishing.com
www.roundfire-books.com

For distributor details and how to order please visit the 'Ordering' section on our website.

Text copyright: David W. Berner 2019

ISBN: 978 1 78904 498 0
978 1 78904 499 7 (ebook)
Library of Congress Control Number: 2019949663

All rights reserved. Except for brief quotations in critical articles or reviews, no part of this book
may be reproduced in any manner without prior written permission from the publishers.

The rights of David W. Berner as author have been asserted in accordance with the Copyright,
Designs and Patents Act 1988.

A CIP catalogue record for this book is available from the British Library.

Design: Stuart Davies

UK: Printed and bound by CPI Group (UK) Ltd, Croydon, CR0 4YY
US: Printed and bound by Thomson-Shore, 7300 West Joy Road, Dexter, MI 48130

We operate a distinctive and ethical publishing philosophy in
all areas of our business, from our global network of authors to
production and worldwide distribution.

Also by David W. Berner

October Song: A Memoir of Music and the Journey of Time

The Consequence of Stars: A Memoir of Home

A Well-Respected Man: A Novel

Night Radio: A Love Story

Accidental Lessons: The Memoir of a Rookie Teacher and a Life Renewed

Any Road Will Take You There: A Journey of Fathers and Sons

There's a Hamster in the Dashboard: A Life in Pets

For Sally, Sadie, Soupy, Hogan, Mike, Dakota, and Sam.

I've seen a look in dogs' eyes, a quickly vanishing look of amazed contempt, and I am convinced that basically dogs think humans are nuts.

—John Steinbeck, *Travels with Charley*

And So It Begins

It was the summer of 1963 and my best friend was moving away. He lived a block up the street in a brick bungalow, and on many summer days after elementary school had let out for the season, Mark and I would build forts on the home's wide stone porch. We draped a bed sheet over an old chair and a couch his parents had planted there, and with our green plastic Army guns we would climb inside, preparing ourselves to battle the Nazi soldiers who would soon be coming over the hill. We played for hours, pretending we were under fire from a determined enemy, an enemy we would always overcome. During a break from the skirmishes, his mother would bring us lemonade. As we refreshed ourselves under the billowing sheet, there beside us standing guard was my dog.

Sally was a tri-colored collie given to me by my grandfather, my mother's dad, just a few months after I was born. "A boy needs to grow up with a dog," he told my mother when he came to the door, the eight-week old puppy in his arms. From the time I could walk, Sally was right there with me. She followed me on walks in the woods. She came along when I visited my grandmother's home a block away. And on that porch up the street on that hot day in August decades ago, Sally was there. Not only keeping an eye out for Nazi soldiers, but also reminding me she would never leave me, even if my friend would soon leave forever.

When you are seven years old, you struggle to understand

the concept of change, that things would not always stay the same. I knew my friend was moving, he told me so, but I could not comprehend what that truly meant. People in my world did not move away. My parents grew up on the same street where I grew up. My grandparents lived a few houses away. My aunt and cousins lived on a parallel street, a five-minute walk from my home. Change—someone leaving—seemed a dreadful concept.

The day of the move, a long, tall truck parked on the street outside Mark's door. Big men moved tables and chairs, box after box, table lamps, dressers, and trunks. Mark and I stood in the front yard and shook hands. "I guess I'll see ya," Mark said. "When?" I asked. Mark did not answer.

On the slow walk home with Sally at my side, I tried not to think about what was happening. *How far could he really be going? Maybe he'd still be at school?* I stroked the top of Sally's head and rubbed behind her ear. She nuzzled against my hip. "You're a good girl," I murmured. I was certain that no matter what was happening with my friend, Sally would stay. She would always be my dog, always be my friend. She was not packing her things into a moving truck that would rumble down the street and out of sight.

About halfway to my house, I stopped and sat in the grass along the sidewalk. I wasn't ready to go home. Sally sat next to me and curled up to rest her head on my knee. For a good while, the two of us silently sat, waiting for my confused feelings to go away. I patted Sally's back. She licked my hand. I hugged her around the neck and held on for a long time. When we started to walk again, we did not head straight home. Instead we took the long way, through the backyards, across the alley, and down another street. We ambled over a hill dotted with evergreen trees and through a stretch of maples near a creek. Time stood still. Sally and I were less than a few tenths of a mile from home, but looking back, we were walking a great distance from one thing and closer to something new. I didn't know this then, but

I believe that time with Sally was my first encounter with the beauty and redemptive power of a contemplative walk, and especially a walk with one's dog. The little boy in me would not have comprehended this, but in time I would realize how that day was my first lesson on how a journey, even a short one, could deliver solace, how you could make things right by putting one foot in front of the other. Kierkegaard—a famous daily walker—once wrote in a letter to his favorite niece who had been struggling with personal problems—"If you just keep walking, everything will be all right." This little boy knew nothing of Kierkegaard. But he knew how he felt after that walk with his dog, his constant companion.

It was a tough day for a little boy, but without Sally, it would have been unbearable. She eased me through the first big change in my life. Sally was there when I realized that nothing would remain, life would forever shift. She was there to hold open the lens a little longer so I could see that a walk, especially with your dog, could heal but also open you up, permit space in the soul's tight chambers, allow your heart to heal.

So here I am, many years later, at the age of sixty and change has been, as it always is for anyone, part of life. I left Pittsburgh to attend college a hundred miles away. I left Pennsylvania and moved to Chicago for a job as a radio journalist. I've married and divorced, and married again. I've had two sons. Children forever change you. I have moved from one state to another. Lived in a dozen houses, apartments, and condos. I've changed jobs. Lost friends and found new ones. Buried family. And over the years have cared for eight dogs, from Sally to Sam, which I share with my wife, Leslie. Sam—a black golden doodle—came into our lives not long after my dog and Leslie's dog, animals we had raised before we met, died of old age. Sam was a few months old when she came to us, and at the same time Sam was figuring out who she was as a young dog in a new home, I was contemplating who I had been and who I wanted to be in my older years. There are mileposts at which one inevitably examines a life—the age of 21, at 30, 40, 50. You celebrate with parties. Sometimes you set goals. Make priorities. You ask questions: What do I believe? What do I cherish? What scares me? What thrills me? At 60 years old, it was a good time to ask again. I was on sabbatical leave from Columbia College in Chicago. This was a good time to reexamine, to put the lens squarely on me and focus on who I was in my late years. It was also a good time to train a dog. Not that Sam needed a lot, she had already been housebroken, but she was in a new home, had new owners, had to adjust to new smells, had to find her place. In essence, she had to reexamine who *she* was. So, what would we do? How would Sam and I do this together?

Walk.

There are plenty of epic foot journeys: Camino de Santiago, the pilgrimage in Spain or The Pacific Crest Trail, all 2600 miles of it. My walks would be local. Mini-adventures. Neighborhood walks. Woods walks. Slow. "It's a great art to saunter," wrote Thoreau. Sam and I would be more like old Henry David; we would ramble, roam, and wander. Literature, art, and philosophy are littered with great walkers, those who believed a good walk lights a creative spark, can heal the soul, repair the heart, can work out a problem, can illuminate the world around us and ourselves. Thoreau was one of those walkers, so was Rimbaud and Twain. There's Joyce, Dickens, and Kierkegaard, of course. It's a long list. It was time *I* joined the list of the famous and the unknown, and I would do it with my dog. Sally was my companion on my first philosophical, contemplative walk and Sam could rekindle what had been lost in the years.

And so it begins, methodically and patiently, my regular walks with Sam. What might we learn from each other, find out about ourselves, and when this season of walking is behind us, who will we be?

The answers will come one walk at a time.

Walk 1
Not Enough Socks in the World

If there is a sock in the house, anywhere in the house, Sam will find it. Sam can't get enough socks. A few days ago, she coughed one up, an entire sock—men's black dress, swallowed whole. I threw it out.

Sam also snatches books. She once brought me a copy of Thoreau's *Walden* from a basement coffee table. Other times it was a screwdriver, a small flashlight, underwear, my wife's blouse. Mind you, she does not chew these items, necessarily. Not most of them. Instead, she finds them intriguing enough to prance around with them and eventually offer each to me. Sam's vet says dogs become attached to items their owner has touched; those items carry the scent, and so the dog holds them close so it can be close to you. It's like a child and its favorite blanket. Think Linus. Still, I can't help wonder, on the day when Sam brought me her leash, if she didn't only want to be close to my scent but was suggesting something more.

Let me tell you a bit about Sam.

My wife's ex brought the dog to his home, expecting it to be hypoallergenic. Golden doodles are said to be. Sam wasn't. Not entirely. Vets say no dog really is; doodles are just less likely to cause symptoms for someone who is allergic. But it didn't work out and Sam needed a new home. We took her in for a test run at our house for two days and I fell in love. She was sweet, attentive, and trained. Expressive eyes. Smart. Within hours, there was little doubt what we would do. Her papers and vet information were in order, and her toys—a rubber bone and an old tennis ball—along with two brushes were collected in a bag and handed over. And now, a year after adopting Sam, we are down a few socks, but all else is good. She's a winner of a dog. And she has shown signs of being a good walker, willing to join me when we have occasionally stepped off. Walking her in the past had mainly been about getting Sam some exercise. Now, it was also about me. When I was younger, I sometimes saw walking as an artistic endeavor, offering a creative boost—time to think, wander, open the mind. However, although I try, I am not the most mindful person. But I would like to be. However, a Zen master I am not. Still, with Sam at my side and the two of us combining our efforts, could I be?

* * *

I have an eye doctor appointment later in the day, so I want to get out early for our first walk. It's a nice March morning; a bit cool now but the early sunshine suggests a rather warmish day ahead. Spring fights the end of winter. You can feel the sun taking over the night's chill. I love the day's first hours. It's as if they are my own, as if I've stolen them from those who have chosen not to awaken this early.

Sam and I immediately head east from the house and Sam, without hesitation, begins to sniff. She is a sniffing machine—a leaf, a tree trunk, parkway grass, the edge of the cement sidewalk. I had forgotten how relentless she is. I read somewhere that a dog's incredible sense of smell is linked to its sense of place. Sniffing gives the dog information about what is nearby, what has been here, and what is coming. Their noses are like our eyes. We look around; they sniff around. And Sam is a world-class sniffer. Her behavior is quite appropriate, however, being keenly aware of what's around us on these walks is part of the point.

It's primary election season in Illinois, so in many of the yards are signs for candidates in the hunt. Although I care about the upcoming election, the signs are interference, a kind of litter. Sam sniffs one of them. It's for candidate Becky Anderson, a democratic hopeful for the local congressional seat. She is family to the owners of the local bookstore. Sam spends a great deal of time smelling up Becky's sign and I let her. The edges of the board, the metal posts. Sniff, sniff, sniff. Maybe she knows something about Becky I don't. Or maybe Sam is trying to decide whom she would vote for, if she could.

We walk two blocks farther east and then head north. In a driveway, a woman in black yoga pants, an oversized blue tossle cap, and big puffy coat loads items into the trunk of a SUV. On the brick wall of the home next to the garage, an Irish flag hangs. The woman spots Sam and me.

"Well, hello puppy."

She had never seen Sam or me before. I had never seen her.

"Someone is Irish," I say, nodding toward the flag.

"My husband's mother was a Callahan," she says.

"My grandmother was a Dugan."

"Ever been?" she asks. "I want to take my husband. I'm the token Dego, so, no biggie for me. But he'd love it."

"So, Irish and Italian family. How are your holidays?"

"Drama," she laughs.

Sam sniffs the tires of the SUV then sits and watches us, as if she's accepting this exchange, as if giving her approval to the conversation and the momentary suspension of our walk.

Sandy introduces herself. She has two young children. One of them is a terror, she says, and she worries it'll be a long time before he calms down. I tell her it took more than a decade for my wild child to settle. She grimaces. Sandy asks about Sam, and Sam appears to know she's being talked about. She stands, nuzzles into me, and looks at Sandy. Her puppy-ness shows—eager, but unsure of what to do with her impatience. I notice her poodle-like curls need brushing.

For several minutes, Sandy and I stand at the end of her driveway talking about Ireland, the Netflix series *The Crown*, how she likes the trees in our neighborhood but is not looking forward to all the leaves that will fall in autumn. At the end, we wish each other a happy St. Patrick's Day and say goodbye. Sam and I walk north again on the sidewalk and I wonder—*without Sam by my side, would I have ever met Sandy—my neighbor just two streets away? Would there have been any other time and place for such an encounter?* She's younger. I'm older. My kids are grown. Hers are little. It was Sam's presence that made it happen. Sam, with her show horse prance and her openness to the world signaled to Sandy that I was okay. I was safe. I was approachable. If I had been walking alone, would it have been different? Sandy may have simply smiled and turned away, a perfunctory glance. She may not have acknowledged me at all.

Early spring flowers are pushing their way through dirt—the green leaves of tulips, daffodils, and hyacinth. Tight tiny blossoms form on the ends the branches of a Magnolia tree. And as we head west and then south toward home, Sam's attention turns to a FedEx truck parked in front of a white brick home. The man in the driver's seat studies a package and turns toward us as Sam delivers a tiny, innocuous bark.

"Nice looking dog," he says, smiling.

"That's Sam," I say. "Say hello, Sam."

She offers another soft bark.

"And she talks, too," the driver says.

"Yeah, you should hear the things she says sometimes."

I turn to our home's driveway and release Sam from her lead. She runs to the back of the house and waits at the gate. I open it and she chases after a green tennis ball in the yard, snatches it in her mouth, and looks directly at me.

Thanks for the walk.

"You're welcome," I say. "It's one of many to come. You and me."

Looking forward to it. One more thing, when I'm ready to come inside, will there be socks?

Walk 2
What We Leave Behind

There are few things less awkward than walking the neighborhood carrying a plastic bag of poop. Nothing dignified about it. There you are, hiking the streets, leash in one hand, and a bag of your dog's stool in the other. At our very first turn, Sam squats. This means I'll be carrying poop in a bag for several blocks.

Like I say, no dignity.

"You couldn't have waited?" I ask.

Sorry, Sam appears to say.

I shake the bag and tie it up tight.

It's late afternoon, a good day, sunny and close to 50-degrees. Not bad for mid-March. Sam's doing a bit of her usual sniffing, and I'm looking around. Robins are out. There's one by the base of a maple tree in the parkway. An old gold-colored Plymouth Fury, circa maybe 1975 or so, remains parked in the next-door neighbor's driveway. I have never seen it on the street or heard its engine churn since moving to the area three years ago. In the distance, I hear children playing. A basketball strikes pavement. All is normal in the neighborhood.

As we make our way along the block, I notice for the first time, a section of the concrete sidewalk where a child has pressed the imprint of a hand, like the hand of a celebrity on the Hollywood Walk of Fame outside Grauman's Chinese Theatre. The hand imprint has been there a long time. So has the sidewalk. And above the hand, scratched in the concrete, is the name Molly.

"Who do you think Molly is?" I ask.

Sam looks at me and appears to wonder, I don't know, but she certainly was here, and she wanted everyone to know it.

Kind of what we all want, to be sure everyone knows we've been here, that we made a mark in the world, small or big. We all want people to recognize we spent time on this Earth.

It's a rather deep thought so early in the walk, and it quickly fades when I realize I'm still holding the bag of poop. Yin and Yang of walking Sam. Introspection, meditative thought … and poop. I wonder, though, if these realities aren't intrinsically connected? My hopes for these walks with Sam are that they open up something fresh, something meaningful each day we head out. But like any endeavor we might consider initially significant, this walk comes along with the utterly mundane, the everyday, the bland realities of living. You cook a romantic dinner and you still have to wash the pots and pans. You step out for a daily meditative, restorative walk, and you must reach down with an open plastic bag and scoop up your dog's excrement.

Cleaning up after Sam is also a symbol of community, isn't it? Sam squats in a neighbor's yard, and you wait patiently to take care of the mess. A neighbor sees you and what does he think? He's a good neighbor. A good guy. He's doing the right thing. Carrying the poop is a badge of honor. And, oddly, at the same time I consider this the deeper meaning of picking up after your dog, I am examining the delicate hand of a child stamped in hardened cement, the hand of Molly, who once found such joy in marking her spot.

The Yin and the Yang.

I think about heading north now, but decide to stay eastbound. And within a short block, I see yet another hand in concrete, and next to it, only a couple of inches away, one more hand. Not the left and the right of one, but the hands of two different people, children. No names this time, but dates have been etched in the concrete. The numbers, however, are unreadable. Too many years have passed.

Sam sniffs the hand imprints.

We make our way one block and then head north, passing empty garbage cans dragged curbside the night before and now left empty and discarded after the work of waste haulers. Some of the cans are overturned. A woman uprights one and rolls it to her garage then disappears inside her home. In a moment, she returns, walking out the front door holding a dog in her arms, cradling it like a child. The dog is white; it looks to be a bulldog of some type—chunky and compact. Sam's ears perk up. The woman carries the dog down three front steps, across the lawn and driveway, and then, as delicate as placing a bouquet of flowers on a dining room table, she lowers the dog to the sidewalk, pats its head, and takes its leash.

"Hello," I say from the other side of the street. "Couldn't help noticing how cautious you were with him."

The woman smiles, adjusts her watchman's cap, and begins to walk south. "Sometimes he needs a little kick-start," she says. "Just a little help."

I laugh. It looked amusing, her transporting the dog and then gently positioning the animal on the ground. But to her, it was an act of kindness, something motherly. Then, as the woman and the dog begin to walk parallel to us, I see how the dog lumbers along, its short, squatty legs, struggling to pull it forward. It is old, tired, and reluctant. But the woman insists. "It's good for you," I hear her say. I'm certain she'll walk him at least the length of the block, taking it slow and steady. She'll be patient. She'll encourage. She'll allow him to do his outdoor duties. She'll smile and praise him. Then, as gently and kindly as she did before, she'll lift the old dog into her arms, and carry it inside her home. She'll offer water and food, and allow him to sleep off the exercise in a soft cotton dog bed. And she will know, and the dog will know, too, that no matter how old he gets, it is not yet time for this dog to give up making its mark on the world.

Sam and I take the corner and head south toward the house. And there, stamped in the sidewalk, is one more child's hand, another symbol of life, another mark on the world, another young person proclaiming their existence. Sam and I stop and take a closer look, and I wonder: If they could, would dogs do the same, mark their paws in wet concrete? Claim their place?

"Sam, how about you, would you cast your paw in the sidewalk?" I ask.

You bet I *would*. That old bulldog would, too. We all want some monument to our lives, proof that we walked out here together.

"Pretty profound, Sam," I say.

Sam steps ahead of me, pulling on her leash to lead us home.

Walk 3
The Walking Dead

Sam is sick. She has thrown up several times, sits alone in the corner of the living room, lethargic and disinterested, showing no signs of being in a walking mood.

Like most dogs, Sam gets into things she shouldn't—the garbage, for one. But she's not a chewer. Still, I am concerned she might have swallowed something bad, really bad, something that would harm her, something dangerous.

Years ago, I had a golden retriever that ate rocks. He would gnaw on small pebbles like hard candy. The vet said as long as he was passing them, it was not a problem. But I should try to keep him from doing that. It wasn't easy. That same dog chomped on tennis balls, and once I thought he had swallowed a large portion of one. After a frantic trip to a 24-hour animal hospital and a series of X-rays, the vet on duty found no tennis ball in the throat or belly. It was scary, though.

And now, with Sam's sickness, my thoughts have gone to the dark side. What if Sam needs surgery? What if … she died? How did I get from a reasonably concerned pet owner to someone preparing to bury his dog?

* * *

It is mid-morning. Sun is bright. Good day for anything outside; a good day for a walk. Sam has improved since yesterday. She has some energy back and I feel alive. So, I plan a long one—one mile to the village downtown, a walk through the neighborhood nearby, and then to the park. Maybe it will be too much for Sam right now, but I'm willing to give it a try. I hope she is, too.

In all the many times I have walked this park, it is only now that I notice the many tributes to the dead. On plaques attached to benches and concrete markers next to saplings are memorials to aunts, grandmothers, and friends. Not just one, or two, but five, six, seven—small markers, like gravestones, with words of solemn remembrance. I am told the park sells these memorials to the grievers as a way to fund the maintenance.

Sam sniffs the words engraved on a plaque tacked to the seatback of a wooden bench near the park's big shelter.

"Who is that, Sam?" I whisper.

Sam's sad eyes look to me.

The woman was Sarah. Sarah Butler. Not far from this marker is another near a growing tree. The name is Zach. A grandmother named Nina is remembered on another bench a few yards away. Lauren is memorialized on a plaque near the monkey bars. Wives, mothers, fathers, and children. The entire park—on bench after bench, next to sapling after sapling—monuments to lives gone. Small tributes. Silent and simple.

Why here? Why this park in the middle of suburban Chicago, next to a middle school, a soccer field, four-bedroom homes?

I walk along the far end of the walkway and out of the park with a gloom surrounding me, as if leaving a wake. Sam appears to have lost the zip in her step. Is it the lingering malaise from not feeling well or is she, too, sad?

We walk west and meet a man with a new puppy—all black, like Sam.

"What kind?" he asks from the other side of the street.

I tell him and I ask about his.

"Lab and poodle," he says "Just two months old."

"Sam will be two years this summer."

"Young," he says, "A lot of life left in both of them."

Sam tugs the leash, showing no signs of illness.

"She's still very much a puppy," the man says.

Yes, she is. Sam has another ten good years, maybe. When Sam's time is up, I'll be an old man. Sam might be my last dog.

"Good luck," I tell the new dog owner. "Looks like you've got a good one there."

He smiles, waves.

Sam and I turn northward. I think about my age. In ten years, I'll be 70.

In less than a block, Sam spots a dog in a front lawn. The dog is black with a white stripe on its nose, brown paws. It's tied to the front entrance banister on a long leash and stands in the middle of the yard, slumped and hunched. It moves only its head to have a look at us. Sam appears to respect the dog's reluctance to engage. She watches, but does not lunge toward it. There is no bark. No whimper.

"Look at the old guy, Sam," I say.

He's lived a good life, Sam must be thinking. But he's tired. So tired.

Around the bend eastward and then south, there's another dog. Big golden retriever. He's prone in the front yard of a brick home, a brown lump in the lawn, facing away from us. The old dog slowly drops its head to the ground between outstretched front paws.

"Hey buddy," I say. The dog does not move. I say it again. Nothing. Deaf, I presume, old and deaf.

I think of the memorials in the park. I think of the names. I think of the people left behind, and the ones who loved them.

We are near home now, and I ask, "Sam, you never think of getting old, do you?"

Sam spots a robin, hopping near the sidewalk. She pays no attention to the question or to me. The robin bounces up a driveway and across a lawn. Sam is locked on it. It's a brand new season and the birds know it. The robins are everywhere now. And Sam is right there with them on this new day, this new beginning. Whatever once ailed her appears to have evaporated. Life has awakened around her on this long walk on another precious day. Sam does not think of sickness, does not think of aging; death is far away, as it should be for the young and the bold and those who trust in immortality.

Walk 4
Crazy Guy

There's a crazy guy in the neighborhood. You might say he's a little … off. Everyone knows it. I believe Sam knows it, too. His home is behind ours on a parallel street. Last summer he decorated his front lawn with bizarre items—a baby carriage, an axe, an inflatable whale—the kind of blow-up toy kids play with in a backyard pool. There once was a plastic life-size goose sitting on the lawn and a pair of snow skis leaning against a tree. Two colored lights framed his driveway—one red and one green, like Christmas, and written in colored chalk on his driveway were messages about a local CBS radio station—*Rock On* and *K-Hits*.

Like I say. Maybe just a little … off.

It is late morning when Sam and I walk by Crazy Guy's home. This time, and the last several times I've been this way, there is nothing in his yard. All the things that had been there before have been cleared away. I wonder if Crazy Guy's wacky lawn ornaments are seasonal?

We move closer to his front walkway and Sam appears more curious. She sniffs the bricks near the driveway and around the plants near the front entrance of his home. Sam is anxious, wary but inquisitive. I have to pull her away so we can keep walking. I look over my shoulder one last time for any strange additions to the yard, but there is nothing. Odd items one week and nothing the next.

Who is this guy?

I have never seen Crazy Guy up close. One time, from a distance, I saw him cutting his grass but that was it. He must be socially odd, uncomfortable with human interaction. Dangerous? I doubt it, but there *was* that axe in the lawn. I wonder if other neighbors have met him, talked to him. Certainly they, too, have noticed the David Lynch-esque set design of his yard. Is it a random act or is he trying to say something, some poetic metaphor? Or is it simply the work of a jumbled mind trying to sort itself out?

As Sam and I pass to the north of the house, Sam looks over her shoulder, just as I did moments before, seemingly longing to confront Crazy Guy, maybe to understand this eccentric and curious man in our neighborhood.

"What do you think, Sam? What about this guy?"

Sam whines.

"Soon, I'm going to have to knock on his door," I say.

Trimmers are scheduled to work on the big old trees in our backyard. They'll be sawing off dead branches. Some tree limbs from Crazy Guy's evergreen trees in the rear of his yard are hanging over the fence into ours and need to be clipped to help allow sun for a garden. Before the trimming is done, I hope to speak with Crazy Guy. It is the neighborly thing to do. I don't want to start knocking off the branches of his trees without talking to him first, even though legally I don't have to okay this with him. I've learned that if the limbs of another's tree are in your yard, trimming them is fair game. But I don't want to do that, and so, this means walking to his front door, ringing the bell, and meeting him, talking to him, looking him in the eye.

Why does this make me uneasy? I like people. I am comfortable with new neighbors. What is it?

There's been a lot in the news lately about the awful fix our country is in. There appears to be more contempt than ever before, more ignorance and tension between political parties, between races, between religions, between the young and the old, between regions of the country, between men and women. Massive protests over terrible gun violence, school shootings, and sexual harassment. A divided country reels from ignorance, the kind of ignorance that can breed uncertainty and hatred. People's words are harsh; there are snarls and angry screams, taunting and nasty faceless accusations on social media. Reading the news has become an exercise in sorrow. And the world's dreadful mood is on my mind, coming in and out of focus, as Sam and I take our walk. It's pervasive, hard to ignore.

Then it hits me. I am part of the problem.

As we turn the corner to head east and then south, I tighten Sam's leash and pull her toward me, squat to her level, and look in her dark eyes.

"Why do you bark at some dogs and not others?" I ask. "Think about it, Sam. You've sneered and barked at another dog that walks by us, but as soon as you meet, go nose to nose, sniff each other, get to know one another a bit, there is no more growling, is there?"

Sam tilts her head as if realizing something.

"When you stand on the living room chair and bark out the window at the mailman, showing all of your anger, are you just barking from ignorance?" I ask. "When you met him that one time in the front yard, what did you do? You licked his outstretched hand; you pined for a pat on the head. Have you forgotten?"

Sam hangs her head and looks at the ground as if ashamed.

"Me too, Sam," I say. "Me too."

We turn around and head back from where we'd been, crossing the street, over the parkway grass, and onto the sidewalk toward Crazy Guy's place. I again shorten Sam's lead and take the concrete sidewalk to the stairs. Two days' worth of newspapers are on the stoop. A flyer for a local landscaper has been tightly rolled and slipped into the handle of a sun-faded brown screen door. I try the doorbell, a black button worn from age. No sound. I knock on the screen door. On the window of the main door are torn and faded stickers—one for Western Illinois University and another for the Magellan Project, the 1989 NASA Jet Propulsion Laboratory, an exploration of Venus that lasted through the mid-1990s. I wait and rap again, noticing the soiled lace curtains covering the door's window.

I want to introduce myself. Introduce Sam. I'll look him in his eyes. I'll smile. I'll ask his name. I'll shake his hand.

Sam sits on the small stoop. I knock one more time and listen for stirring in the house, something that tells me there is life beyond the door. But there is nothing, no sound and no one.

"Not this time," I tell Sam, taking to the steps. I look back to the door one more time, as if expecting to see someone. Instead, there are only the newspapers in clear plastic bags on the concrete. I pick them up and tuck them inside the rusted mailbox on the porch. Sam watches, as if approving of my gesture. "One of these days," I add, "one day you'll get to meet Crazy Guy."

Sam and I walk slowly to the sidewalk. I allow her to sniff the tree in the parkway near Crazy Guy's driveway and wait patiently. *He must be at work,* I think. *Sleeping after working the night shift? Maybe he's taken some time away. I'll come back tonight, maybe tomorrow. Another day, soon.*

Turning the corner toward home, I wonder how many neighbors have knocked on Crazy Guy's door. How many have seen him, said hello, offered a wave. I'm certain I would not recognize him if I met him on the street, at the grocery store. And now, after anticipating an encounter, I am disappointed. I want to meet him. I want to know for sure that he is as crazy as our imaginations have allowed, or better yet, that he is no crazier than any of the rest of us on this street and in this neighborhood.

Sam and I are nearly home now, and from across the street I see a woman pushing a baby carriage. She holds a red leash and at the end of it is a small dog—white and fluffy. It bounces toward us with great purpose, happy with the world, and when the dog sees Sam, it tugs hard toward her. Sam tugs, too. Each wants to be close to the other, to snort and smell, to look in each other's eyes. There are no whines, no barks—not a yap, not a bark, not a sneer.

"They want to say hello," the woman says, "and it looks like nothing is going to stop them."

I smile.

"I'm Margaret, by the way," she says.

"David, and this is Sam," I say, nodding toward her.

"Molly," she says, offering her dog's name.

The two dogs nuzzle and sniff. Tails twitch. We have to pull them away from one another to be on our separate ways.

"And to think they'd never met before," I say as we start to walk away.

"And not one hesitation," the woman says.

The two of us step away pulling our dogs along.

When we arrive home, I freshen Sam's water bowl and give her a small doggie treat.

And the next day, Sam and I return to Crazy Guy's door. We knock once. Twice. And wait. But again, there is no answer. As we step down from the stoop, I notice the house across the street. On the front door there appears to be a giant cardboard bunny rabbit in full spring regalia. A lace of plastic spring flowers— pink and yellow and blue—is draped around the entranceway, and in the yard, a woman, an older lady in her 70s or maybe 80s. On her head, she wears a pair of big fluffy rabbit ears—pink and white—and she places large plastic multi-colored eggs on the muted green grass of her lawn, one after another, dozens of them, each about two feet apart. The yard is awash in the colors of Easter, which is only days away. I can't help noticing the woman's smile, the joy in her work, and although she does not see me, I smile back. And Sam watches as I watch. Sam, too, sees how this woman might appear to others, walking around in those floppy cottontail ears, planting plastic eggs on a spring day.

"Crazy person, Sam," I whisper. "Simply a crazy person."

In a day or two, Sam and I will return to Crazy Guy's house. We will knock again, and we finally will meet him. And in a brief conversation on Crazy Guy's porch, I'll ask if he's okay with the tree trimming, and ask about his zany lawn ornaments, and he'll dismiss all of it only to mention the crazy lady across the street. She's a little weird, he'll say. Those rabbit ears, he'll say. And I'll smile, and Sam will smile, too, and together we will wish each another a Happy Easter.

Walk 5
The Longing

I flip the switch on the small space heater and the green light comes on. The unit is just powerful enough to warm the 5x8 space. The idea is to get things going, go do something else, maybe make coffee, and in fifteen minutes or so the temperature should be just right. There's a light drizzle this morning, abnormally raw and chilly for the first part of April, even for Chicago. It is the kind of cold and damp that seeps below the skin. Earlier this morning, just after sunrise, I was comfortably warm, resting in bed reading the last five pages of *Winter*, one of four books of essays by Karl Ove Knausgård, the Norwegian writer who's receiving attention from all over the world for his six-volume autobiographical novel *My Struggle*. I finished the essay book and while still in bed, found myself wondering how writing about such seemingly random and mundane things like safety reflectors, one's nose, stuffed animals, and sugar could be so fascinating.

It's a short walk, about thirty yards, from the back of the house to the shed, a little writing space I built for myself a year ago. I nailed barn wood to the walls, tiled the floor, painted. It's a modest place with electricity and light, a single window, a desk, and a perfect place for some of my books, the ones I cherish the most. I place *Winter* on the shelf next to *Autumn*, the first book in the series.

The blinds on the door are open just enough to allow a bit of light in, and to present to me an image. Between the white slats, I see Sam standing on the other side of the rear entrance to the main house, her nose against the glass, her breath fogging up the window enough that I could write her name with my finger. She knows there will be a walk today. I told her so before coming to the shed. Whenever I put shoes on or reach for my coat, Sam stands to attention, anticipating travel, and if the readying means there is to be a walk, I let her know. But I also let her know when she may have to wait. This is one of those times. But Sam's look of longing this morning is tough to ignore—those eyes ache. I too, look forward to the walk, light rain or not, but first, there's the writing. It waits for me. It expects me to be in the shed. The need to write—to sit and think through a project, an observation, a story—is difficult to dismiss. But now there's Sam at the door.

Sam and I take the sidewalk south and make the turn at the first intersection. Across the street, I see a dog in a window, its face up against the glass of a large bay window looking out over the lawn of a corner lot. Like Sam watching me from the back door, this dog is observing our every move. It appears most interested in Sam, watching Sam sniff wood chips left by a crew that had recently taken down a parkway tree. The dog's eyes follow as Sam examines the trunk of another still-standing tree. And the dog watches Sam lift her nose into the wind as she catches the scent of something interesting. Sam either does not see this dog in the window or pays no mind. But I do. I see its tan and white face, its dark eyes. And I see the longing. Not envy or jealousy. No, I think it's certainly longing. The dog wants something more than it currently has—it wants to be outside, to be with Sam, to smell spring, to receive a pat on the head from the man walking the neighborhood.

Sam and I head east and the dog's eyes follow until they can no longer.

What is longing? The romantic poets have always linked it to love. But I think it's more than that. I stop at the corner and pull Sam close. I ask her to sit and she does. On my phone I search Google. Poems about longing. There is Shelley, Keats, Shakespeare, Dickinson, and a poet I am not familiar with: Michael Ondaatje. He's from Sri Lanka and Canada, Wikipedia tells me. I read that he has won the Booker Prize, and now I am mildly embarrassed that I don't know of him. In another link there is a quote from his novel *The Cat's Table*.

We all have an old knot in the heart we wish to untie.

"That's it!" I say. Sam snaps her attention toward me. "It's okay, girl. Just looking up something." Sam's eyes remain on me as if waiting for an explanation for my exclamation. I'm not sure I can give her one that would make much sense.

Longing is such a complicated emotion. But Ondaatje's quote helps define it. His words capture the soft desire of wanting something that is missing, out of reach, impossible to determine. Ondaatje suggests the "knot" is "old"—but maybe not. Maybe the knot is just simply longing itself. We all have a "knot." We all have longing in our hearts—maybe from birth—something we are forever trying to understand and untangle.

Maybe dogs are trying to do the same thing.

Sam and I pass the first parallel street and continue east to the next then head north. The rain remains light; sometimes it stops completely, so we are in no rush. And with that, I slow down even more, allowing Sam to sniff everything she wants, anything that interests her—clumps of early spring grass, a discarded small plastic bag from a convenience store, a small limb that had fallen from a tree to the parkway. I remember a veterinarian telling me that while we walk for fitness, fresh air, or to get from one place to another, dogs have a different purpose. We tend to walk quicker and with resolve. The dog, however, wants to familiarize or reacquaint itself with the surroundings, so they want to walk much slower. In the natural order of things, a dog's preferred pace is a meandering stroll. And to come along, to be a true companion of the walk, the human must slow down and consider what the dog wants, not what the walker wants.

"I don't want you longing for anything, Sam," I say with a smile as she sniffs a cluster of brown wet leaves left over from autumn. There is clearly something exciting there, so I summon my patience. I wait. It's okay.

We move slowly northward with frequent stops for snorts of curiosity. At the turn, a dog—a tan Labrador mix—stands near the garage door of a home. It sees us and with its unwavering eyes, walks slowly to the end of the driveway. The dog is not tethered, but there is likely an electric fence or very good training at work here. It stands still now; only its head moves to keep its eyes on us. There is no bark, no whimper or growl. Like the dog in the window at the start of our walk, it only watches. Longing.

Sam appears disinterested. There's no pull to move closer, only minor curiosity before Sam shifts her focus to a small group of robins hopping across a lawn.

"You don't see him over there?" I ask.

Sam looks at me and returns to the birds.

"I'll take that as a no."

We rarely see those around us longing beyond their daily existence. If we did we would reveal vulnerability, and that is uncomfortable for humans. Dogs must find it uncomfortable too, apparently. All that longing lost in the fog, in the misty rain, in our diverted attention.

On the southward walk home, just around the corner from where landscapers had freshened mulch in the front lawn of a newly renovated ranch home, Sam suddenly becomes playful. She uses her teeth to grab a small stick that had fallen from a parkway tree, and teases me with it. I reach for it; she pulls away. I reach again and she snaps back. Sam spins and falls on her back, rubbing her body against the ground, gnawing on the stick. She's happy. She has a toy. She's outside. She's with her best friend.

Walk 6
I'm So Pretty

The dog has a beard. It hangs straight down from his chin some six inches. And on top of his head is the K-9 version of a man bun, the dog's black hair pulled up and tied tight with a rubber band. This is a hipster dog, lying on the wooden floor of Murphy's Bleachers just outside Wrigley Field in Chicago, the local tavern most associated with the Cubs. Seeing the dog, any dog, here is not unusual. It's a dog-friendly establishment. Still, this dog is different.

I'm here for a friend's book launch. It's a collection of stories from long-suffering Cubs fans who were finally able to celebrate a World Series win a couple of years ago. But it's the dog that has most of my attention. More than the former Cubs players here for the event, more than the former Cubs ball girl, more than the old friends who have come to buy a book.

Sam is not with me today. She's at home. But she's on my mind as I drink a pint and eat quesadilla at a small round table near the pub's entrance. *Would Sam have tolerated the hairstyle this dog has? And what would be the equivalent for a female like Sam? Purple hair? Highlights? A shoulder tattoo? And this bearded dog—is he embarrassed?* Clearly the owner wants to give the dog a unique style, but, it seems, this comes at the dog's expense. He's getting plenty of attention from anyone who enters Murphy's. Look at that dog, they say. But I'm not sure the dog wants the notoriety. Or maybe he's just used to occasional ribbing. I swallow my beer. If I were the bearded dog, I consider, I'd be mortified.

In three days, Sam goes in for grooming. She needs it. Doodles don't shed, and that's a good thing. But their hair is easily matted no matter the frequency of brushing. Sam's hair is matted around the elbows and on her chest. And, she smells. I wouldn't say this to her face, but a lot of playing in the backyard, rolling in the grass, and the nature of her hair has resulted in a rather unpleasant scent, a bouquet of staleness and an old wool sweater. Sam's hair is like Velcro; it catches everything—small sticks, leaves, and clumps of dirt stick to her. Picking them out of her hair is a daily occurrence. She is work. Soon, however, Sam will be spruced-up with a nice bath and a good trim, and the results will give the world a much more pleasant looking and smelling beast.

I drink the last of the beer, chew the last cheesy tortilla, pay my bill, and as I exit, I pat the bearded dog's head.

"I hope all the other dogs in here aren't laughing at you," I whisper.

* * *

It's the day before the grooming appointment, and Sam and I go for a walk in the forest preserve. She's looking ratty, still smells, and can barely see me through the hair that hangs over her eyes.

"Good thing I have you tethered. You can't see where the hell you're going," I say, stepping out the back door and connecting the lead to her collar.

Sam is in the moment, she knows a walk is *right now*, imminent; she's present and mindful with no knowledge or nervous anticipation of what will come tomorrow. And I'm not going to tell her.

Nearly every woman I have known has been a bit anxious at times before going to a stylist. My wife can be. She might fret over length and shades of highlights. Men, too, are nervous at the barber, but in my experience, it's not at the same level. A little around the ears is not difficult enough to prompt a level of unease. Still, considering human phobias over grooming, I can understand Sam's probable disquiet. I hope the walk on the trails might take if off her mind.

It's a sunny day, warmer than it has been. Not too many cars in the parking lot. And as we start along the river trail, birdsong fills the air. I spot a bright cardinal far up in a tall maple that has yet to sprout its leaves. It's one of those spring days that reminds you how much you love the change of seasons. This enlivens me. But Sam is not necessarily with me on this. She appears tired. Head down. Not as excited about the walk as she usually is. Maybe it's been too long since we've been to the forest. Maybe she's simply familiarizing. Maybe she's thinking about the grooming.

The woods are mostly brown but there is simple beauty here. It'll be weeks before green takes over, so today I can see through the scrub and brush. Squirrels scurry. They are easy to spot. This would normally alert Sam. But she is not interested. She sees them, but there's no pull to chase. Instead, Sam walks slowly and sniffs the trail's edge.

A jogger passes. He says nothing, focused on his trek. Then a woman passes dressed in wool, a big hat, and gloves. Overkill, it appears, for the warming weather. She smiles. Sam ignores them both. Sam is not herself; she's less attentive and she's not angling for affection, which is almost always the case when someone walks by. I'm now certain she must be thinking about the coming haircut.

We spend an hour on the trail and at the end of the walk near the office of the nature center we spot an older man, dressed in a flannel shirt and a heavy microfiber vest. He carries a green water bottle.

"That's a big dog," he says. There's a hint of an accent. Czech?

"Actually, she has a medium build for a doodle," I say.

He tilts his head.

"She's a mix of black poodle and golden retriever," I add.

"Yes, the hair. It's like a poodle."

Sam sits on the trail. She pants and stretches her head out to smell the man. She growls softly, not aggressively.

"Unsure of me, huh?" the man says.

Sam's tail begins to wag. The man pats her head.

"I hate when they cut poodles all foofoo," he continues.

Sam's ears perk up.

"Not going to happen to her," I say, offering a reassuring scratch behind Sam's ear.

"There's a reason for that foofoo stuff," the man says. "Poodles were first bred as retrievers, bird dogs. The hair was so dense, the owners cut them close, leaving the puff balls around their joints and ears to keep them warm, but the rest was cut to help them dry off when they came out of the cold water."

"Really?" I want to believe the story.

"But of course, women like the look, so people still groom them in that silly way."

"I didn't know that."

"All dogs were working dogs somewhere along the line."

"I wonder what the first poodles back then thought of that hairstyle."

"I'm certain they hated it." The man laughs. "Just like they do now."

I scratch again behind Sam's ear.

"I like your dog's haircut better," he adds.

I think I hear Sam sigh. But does this man know she needs a good grooming?

"Enjoy your walk," I say. Sam stands erect, and turns to walk toward the car. Her step has a little bounce.

* * *

On the way to the groomer, I roll down the rear passenger side window and Sam sticks her head out. The wind attacks her hair like an ocean storm blows a palm tree's fronds. The gusts make her lower lip twitch. For several miles, Sam remains at the window. Her hair is tousled and sticks up on the top of her head. She looks like The Rolling Stones' Ronnie Wood.

We arrive and I open the car door to allow Sam out to the parking lot. She appears excited, anticipating something good and fun, and walks through the door with the eagerness of a child on a play date.

Jackie enters the room and Sam shrinks against my leg.

"I think she just realized what's up," I say.

Jackie is gentle, sweet. She squats to Sam's level and attempts to stroke the top of her head, but Sam cowers.

"Maybe she's thinking about the grooming we had done before we found you," I say to Jackie.

A past groomer scolded me for not properly brushing Sam, telling me Sam was so matted that the grooming might have to be razor close. The final cut was comical. When I saw Sam afterward, I couldn't help laugh. She was hideous; she looked ridiculous. She was shaved to the skin, a tuft perched on the crown of her head, her tail was bushy and out of proportion with the rest of her body. She was a Q-tip, a big, black Q-tip.

"It was traumatizing," I say.

"Awe," Jackie sighs. "Dogs definitely are sensitive to the way you see them."

My father gave me buzz cuts when I was a kid. Down to the nubs. I was in second grade when I got the first one. It wasn't the neat, military crew like Sergeant Carter on The Gomer Pyle Show. This was a skinhead shave. I wanted to wear a hat forever.

I shorten Sam's leash and gently tug her closer to Jackie. She pets Sam's head. "It's okay," Jackie says. I hand her the lead and rub Sam's back. "Just a little clean up," I say. Jackie leads Sam to the door to the back room. At first, Sam pulls to escape but with coaxing she moves forward and does not look back.

* * *

Two hours later, on my return drive to the groomer's, someone on the radio mentions that it's National Pet Day. What a day to damage your dog's confidence with a bad haircut, I think. But I rebalance. It'll be okay. Really, it will. Jackie's good. She knows Sam frets about how she looks. And last time, she did a nice job. The bigger question is not what everyone else thinks of the haircut, but what Sam thinks of it.

Sam's not quite ready. Another fifteen minutes, I'm told. So, I sit in the lobby and read. The book is Steinbeck's *Travels with Charley*, a classic. I first read it many years ago and with my new summer walks underway, I've decided to revisit it. Besides, Charley was a poodle, Sam's distant cousin in the dog world, so it seems fitting. The photo of Charley on the front suggests a well-groomed animal. Steinbeck apparently did a better job than I have.

Jackie emerges, Sam by her side.

"She's all ready to go," Jackie says.

Oh my, I think. Oh my.

Sam is not foofoo, but she is unmistakably poodle. I do not laugh. I do not laugh.

"There were some knots behind one ear and she was pretty dirty," Jackie says. "Lots of chunks in her paws. She likes the mud, doesn't she?"

"Hey girl," I say. Sam twists and turns and crashes into me with enthusiasm. "Mud is a good thing, it seems."

"I had to go a little shorter on the body than I did last time," Jackie says.

I run my hand on Sam's back. Her hair is the texture of a mink coat. The curls are gone. She smells like oranges.

"She is so patient." Jackie smiles.

"I can see your eyes, Sam," I say. Her dark eyes are alert. She looks to me as if it is the very first time. "No more Ronnie Wood." And she's not a Q-tip. The new cut is a little long on the sides and ears, and this has her looking a little like Derek Smalls, the bassist from Spinal Tap.

I do not laugh. I do not laugh.

I pay Jackie, tip her, and make another appointment for three months out. On the way home, Sam leans out the window into the wind, just as she did earlier. The white neckerchief she has been given to wear, a girly one with little purple and red hearts, flaps in the breeze. And when we return home, I take her for a quick walk around the block, a kind of runway strut, you might say. There's bounce in Sam's steps. She sees two young girls playing basketball in a driveway and pulls toward them. One spots Sam and smiles. Sam pulls harder toward her. Look how pretty I am, Sam says. I am very pretty today. But the girl quickly turns away and returns to the hoop and her friend. Hey, Sam says, don't you see how pretty I am? I am so pretty. And I smell absolutely fantastic. Yes. I am oh, so pretty.

Walk 7
You Can't Always Get What You Want

Sam and I trek a different journey today. South to the train tracks, around the bend, and then north along a parallel street. And more than anything, for whatever reason, I notice turtles. Stone turtles. Concrete. Lawn ornaments placed in the front yards and gardens—small ones and big ones, the size of raccoons. There are the usual stone yard adornments—the bunnies, the nymph and her pail of water, the gnome. But turtles outnumber them. This is not to say every house has stone knick-knacks in the yard, but it is strange to see all the turtles.

Sam pays no attention until we close in on one particular yard. But it's not a turtle that catches her eye.

My mother's yard at our home in Pennsylvania when I was growing up was decorated with patches of flowers. Mom did not take to tchotchke in her garden. *The flowers are the stars*, she would say. She wanted the simplicity of floral beauty. But my father wanted a backyard waterfall, one of those cascading kinds, the flowing water produced by a small pump. He never got the waterfall. My mother never agreed. But she did okay a birdbath in one narrow section of the garden. Dad painted the bowl's base aqua blue and he attached a plastic cardinal on the edge of the bath. The fake bird scared off the real birds, and so the birdbath became a water bowl for the dog. Our family pet—a standard rough collie, named Sally—would often stand before the bath to quench her thirst and my father would refill it with the garden hose. This is not what my mother had in mind when she said yes to the birdbath, especially when Sally would trample her way through a patch of lilies to get to it. Still, my mother tolerated the birdbath and my father loved it.

There is no birdbath in the yard where Sam's interest piques. In fact, at this point in the walk I have not seen a single garden water basin. Maybe they're out of style. Instead, Sam's attention is on a very large concrete frog, the size of a cocker spaniel puppy with big bulging eyes, sitting in a row of mulch under a bay window. It is painted several colors—green, blue, red—big and bold. Sam yanks on the leash and offers a low snarl.

On the ground around the frog are foot-high metal mushrooms, like something from Alice in Wonderland. They line the walkway. And to the right, under a second bay window, are two turtles made of light-colored concrete. Yes, more turtles. But it is the frog that has every bit of Sam's focus. Maybe it's the size and its rather menacing stare.

"The frog is not real, you know?" I say.

Sam produces another low growl. But I'm unsure if she is considering an attack or simply wants to investigate a possible playmate. Dogs snap at another animal, sometimes a person, only to sniff them out and discover they are more worthy of friendship than scorn.

Sam moves closer. She angles next to the frog and her tail stiffens, a sign of safety or protection. Then the tail begins to wag. Sam sticks her nose at the frog's base.

"So, now you like the frog?"

Sam looks at me, as if to gain my acceptance at the choice of a friend. She returns to sniffing. Tail still wagging.

"You can't take it home," I say.

There have been times on our walks when Sam has found a ball or a child's toy in a yard and has snatched it in her teeth, as if the rule of the game finders, keepers works in the dog world. The desire for that ball or toy is strong enough to spark a degree of larceny. Sam doesn't appear to be trying to steal the frog, but it wouldn't surprise me if she attempts it, given more leash and her penchant for what can be found in neighborhood lawns.

In the end, we all want what we want. Dad wanted a waterfall. Sam may want a frog. And sometimes, like Dad and Sam, getting what it is we want is out of reach. Sometimes it's the big things — love, companionship, and contentment — sometimes it's a silly frog in a garden. What we hope for is that somewhere along the road, all of us are able to get at least what we need.

Walk 8
The Young and the Old

I am sipping wine at a vineyard near Portland and Sam is throwing up in Chicago.

Sam had puked on the kitchen floor and then several times on a bedroom carpet, and now she is being fed only rice, hoping this will settle her stomach. I learn of her troubled belly by way of a text from my ex-wife, who, along with my son have been watching Sam while Leslie and I are away. We were married seven months ago, but because of my teaching schedule at the college, Leslie and I waited until April and my sabbatical to honeymoon and travel Oregon's coast, its forests, and the wine country in the Willamette Valley. Now we are 2000 miles away and our dog is sick.

Sam is sharing space with another dog in a new house, playing and running at the dog park, sleeping in a different place, and like many of us while on vacation or traveling, her constitution has become unbalanced. This is what I believe. But my mind goes to the dark side. Did she get into something? Eat something she shouldn't have? I try to dismiss my worry. *She's not even two years old yet*, I remind myself. Sam is a young, healthy dog. Her throwing up is like an over-excited child eating too much pizza and cake while attending a kid's birthday party at Chuck E. Cheese's. Sam is partying; she's on vacation. Like that child, Sam will be fine in time. Her youth will get her through it. This is what I tell myself.

* * *

The Oregon trip is a more than 600-mile tour that includes a stop at a friend's home north of Salem. In the early morning after the first night of our stay, while both of our wives are still asleep, my friend and I talk over coffee.

"So, what are you noticing?" my friend asks.

"Noticing?"

"Getting older. I'm creaking more in the morning. Taking longer to get going," he says. "And I'm losing my hearing."

"Really?"

"Yeah," he sighs. "My wife wants me to get it checked."

"Certainly, I'm finding my flexibility is low," I say, ignoring my friend's concerns about hearing. "I need to work on getting loose."

My friend and I are about the same age, early 60s. We are both relatively active. He used to run marathons. I never have. If it counts, I ran two 5Ks ten years ago, but I have always hated running. But I do walk when I play golf, hike now and then, and there are my walks with Sam. But I could always do better.

"Age just wears on you," he adds.

That night, while trying to fall asleep, I think about my friend's words. There's been a lot of walking and hiking in Oregon—the Rogue River Trail near Union Creek, the long walk around the lake in Bend in the shadow of snow-covered mountains, the five-mile hike at Smith Rock watching rock climbers cling to vertical stone cliffs. Age may "wear on you" as my friend says, but I'm pushing back as best I can. Someone important once said or wrote, "There's nothing like a mountain for helping you remember." This seems most appropriate now. Wasn't I forty years old just yesterday? Sometimes I feel forty. I do tonight.

In the hazy minutes just before sleep takes over, my mind wanders and I think of Sam. How is she doing? Is she better? Have there been more episodes of throwing up? I'm troubled by how we left Chicago five days ago. I had forgotten to say goodbye to Sam. We had agreed to leave her at the house to be picked up later by my son to take to the home he shares with his mother. But the morning of our departure, Leslie and I ordered an Uber ride to the airport, and when it arrived, we hurried with the luggage, and I did not kiss Sam on the forehead, did not give her a hug, did not tell her we'd be back. It's a silly thought. I know Sam is in good hands; I know she has everything she needs and more. But is she well? I want to take her for a walk right now. I want to venture out. And then I wonder: Do I walk Sam for her or for me? Do I do it to ward off the creeping menace of age? Are the walks to keep Sam young or to keep *me* young? It's been said that walking—moving the body made for motion—is an act of living. I guess that's why the two of us walk—to live.

Before too long, I am asleep.

* * *

The day after our return to Chicago, Sam and I step out in the early morning. It's cool, sunny, quiet. We plan a short walk, just enough to brush off the long flight and to reacquaint my body with the time zone. For Sam, this walk is a welcome home. She is showing no signs of the earlier sickness and she has the usual spring in her step, that familiar strut.

We head east and then north, and up ahead I see a man and a dog. They are walking slowly, methodically. It didn't take much effort to catch up to them and now we are just fifty yards behind. I know this dog. It's the old golden retriever that I've seen resting, motionless, on its owner's lawn. This elderly dog— overweight, certainly arthritic, and apparently deaf—is slogging forward. The dog's walker stays patient, moving unhurriedly and deliberately, allowing the lead to stretch out as far as it can and the dog to go wherever and however it wants along the grassy parkway. Sam and I take a turn east again and they move in the opposite direction. But as we part, I can see the walker's face. He's a young man, maybe in his early 20s. He appears tired, for it is only 6:30 in the morning. But yet he is content somehow, a young man with an old dog, tolerant and understanding of his friend's labored march, aware of what the dog must remember — those long-ago hikes when its legs moved with athletic ease and its paws touched — if only momentarily — soft, damp grass. I'm not sure the young man sees us, Sam and me, as we move away. But if he does, I wonder what he thinks. Is he aware of the metaphor, the coincidence of a young man and an old dog, crossing paths with an old man and a young dog? Maybe it is only me who ponders this, the one looking for meaning somehow. The young and the old are endlessly crossing trails, touching one another's lives, aware and thoughtful of each other, or finding frustration in the recklessness of youth and the deficiencies of age.

The young man and his dog disappear around the corner, and Sam and I head for home. I'm certain her heart is beating like that of a playful girl, a rhythm only the young can endure, as she dances, lunges, and wrenches hard on her leash to chase a squirrel darting up a maple tree.

Walk 9
I'm Mad at You

Sam is on my shitlist.

"Damn it, Sam! Get over here!" I yell, fighting to be heard above the clunk and grind of a lawn aerator.

It's a warm early afternoon. One of the members of the crew we have hired to aerate our yard, the mess that it is, is walking behind a loud, hefty machine made to produce Magic Marker size holes in the ground. I'm told those holes help give oxygen to the roots and promote growth. We'll see about that. Right now, this doesn't matter. What matters is Sam. She is twirling around the man who operates the engine. Back and forth. Back and forth. She jumps and barks, and performs doggie pirouettes in between the yelps.

"Sam! No one wants to play!"

The man ignores her.

"Damn it, Sam!"

Sam disregards me like a defiant child. She stares at me, still as a photographic image. She looks at the man. She looks at the moaning machine. She looks at me, again. And it's back to her dance.

"Son of a bitch!"

I don't often get mad at Sam. Sometimes she plays a game where she stands at the door apparently wanting to come in the house from the backyard, but when I open the door, she runs. It's annoying. And I think she knows it. Pleasures in it, somehow.

But this aeration tango is new.

After nearly twenty minutes of chasing Sam, scolding her, coaxing her, pleading with her, switching between being irate and feigning disinterest, she gives up, but only after the worker slides his machine into the back of his white pickup truck, smiles at me, and waves goodbye.

"I am so mad at you!" I grab Sam by the collar. Opening the house door, I yank her inside. "Don't even look at me," I say. Sam stands in the kitchen, her tongue long and slippery, dripping drool. Exhausted. She lowers her eyes.

For the next hour, I snub her. Don't acknowledge her. It's a ridiculous thing I'm doing. I know it. Childish. Would I act this way if I were mad at my sons, my wife—ignore them? Still, anger has the best of me.

On a walk earlier in the day, Sam and I spent some time near a playground in the neighborhood. There's a sign posted in the grass advertising summer pool passes for the season. Sam stood next to it as if to ask if I would sign her up. "The tug of summer is strong, isn't it?" I think of this while I sit in a living room chair, simmering with ire. Sam is stretched out on the hardwood, sleeping. It pisses me off that she is so content. Pool pass, I think. You don't deserve a damn pool pass.

Later that evening, Leslie confronts Sam.

"Do you know how mad he is at you?" she whispers. She crouches to Sam's level and looks her in the eye. "You need to apologize."

Leslie then walks Sam to me and has her sit before the chair. "Sam wants to say something to you," Leslie says.

"Oh really?" I ask.

"We had a talk," Leslie says, "and Sam knows she was wrong. She is ready to say she's sorry."

I'm not really mad anymore. Haven't been for a while. I try not to laugh, realizing how silly this exchange has now become, the two of us talking to a dog like this. Still, I ask, "What do you have to say for yourself, Sam?"

Sam's eyes focus on the floor. She looks up at me for a second, and then away again.

"She's sorry," Leslie says, smiling.

"You made me crazy today, girl," I say and pat her on the head. Sam then crawls up in the adjacent chair, rests her head on its arm, and gazes out the bay window as if everything is, and always has been, right with the world.

Time passes and after Sam is fed for the night, she makes her way to the basement. That usually means she's rummaging around in the laundry room for socks or underwear to bring to us. But this time, it is not a Gold Toe or a pair of Hanes. In Sam's mouth is a box of one dozen Titleist golf balls, the entire blue box, tight between her teeth.

"Thinking about nine holes?" I ask as she stands before me.

And now I know. The pool pass, and the golf balls, and the relentless chasing after the aerator, a machine that signifies yard care for a coming, warmer season. Sam is pining for summer. She, like all of us, is done with the cold and the snow, done with weather that keeps her from spending lots of time outside and sometimes from a walk. Sam is a kid waiting for the last day of school.

The next morning, Sam and I step outside early. You might call it a makeup walk. There's a cool breeze, but you can tell it will eventually be a warm day for early May. I hear a mower in the distance cutting grass somewhere and tulips are blooming along the walkway at the house near the corner. We head for the coffee shop a half-a-mile away near the train station. I buy a cappuccino to go and a blueberry muffin, and sit on a bench next to the tracks, feeding Sam bite size treats, and I tell her I am sorry about the other day. "I promise," I say, "never to stay mad at you that long again." Sam sniffs the breeze. *Summer is close,* she must think. *It won't be long now.*

Walk 10
Signs

When touring Oregon a few weeks ago, Leslie and I drove past a row of rundown, wood frame houses on a remote rural road some twenty miles outside the town of Sisters. In a front yard was a homemade sign. Erected next to a large woodpile, a small American flag and three rusting automobiles, was a large white cardboard placard, a kind of heavy poster board, with the words Black Lives Matter written in dark paint. Slicing across those words was a deep red slash. Next to it was another sign. This one read Gay Rights with another red slash. There were maybe a dozen others in several yards, signs that raged with big, bold writing. Driving past them at fifty miles per hour, we could not read them all. And that was a blessing.

Different kinds of signs are all around me now as Sam and I take an evening walk just before dark. They are nothing like those along the Oregon highway. These are neighborhood signs I have ignored, missed, or disregarded until now. But visions of those Oregon signs resurface as we walk, leaking on me like oil from a massive spill in the waters of a pristine mountain lake, fouling an otherwise heavenly land and the memory of a good trip. The neighborhood signs do not evoke the same painful emotions, but they do offer something I may not have noticed if it had not been for what we had seen in Oregon.

Walking Sam, or any dog, is an agreement to interpret the world. The dog, unlike the human, takes in what it is given with a life-affirming awareness. It's the dog's nature, it seems. Sam cannot read these signs, of course, but she still decodes the world in her own way with deep regard and a trust that good will prevail. If she had command of our language, what kind of sign would she post in her lawn? No Cats Allowed. Sniff in Your Own Yard. Pick Up After Your Human. Bark if You Love Bones. I imagine they would be more profound than this, more in tune with a dog's innate sense of what is right, fair, or just. There is no science or hard evidence to this, of course. It is simply what I believe.

Sam and I head west and then south toward the train tracks. In the yards of three adjacent homes, there are signs for security systems, signs announcing installed units that if triggered will alert police. Is there more crime here than I know? Or are the signs only indications of our false fear in a seemingly troubled world, the myth of razor blades in apples on Halloween?

"Are you worried about the neighborhood, Sam?" I ask.

Sam sniffs a dandelion.

Posted to a tree in Crazy Guy's lawn, is a yellow Beware of Dog sign. Crazy Guy does not own a dog. It makes me wonder: *Is he trying to scare people away?* In several other yards are signs touting the accomplishments of high school athletes—baseball teams, lacrosse teams, and tennis players—signs to remind us they are part of something, no matter their abilities. There are signs stuck in the ground near the front doors of the homes of families who send their children to the local Catholic schools— Notre Dame and St. Isaac Jogues. Outside another house, a sign of caution. White and green lettering warn of potentially harmful chemicals sprayed on the grass to keep the lawn green and the crabgrass out. I pull on Sam's leash to keep her away. Through all of these signs, I see a neighborhood wrapped in pride—pride in home, pride in their children. It is so very human to offer the world the stories of what we love, what we cherish—safety, family, even the greenness of a yard. Yet, I wonder what is missing.

Before seeing the unsettling signs in Oregon, Leslie and I had spent a couple of days in the town of Bend where a different kind of sign was visible in the yards of houses on nearly every street we walked.

IN OUR AMERICA
All people are equal.
Love Wins.
Black lives matter.
Immigrants & refugees are welcome.
Disabilities are respected.
Women are in charge of their bodies.
People & planet are valued over profit.
Diversity is celebrated.

This is what I wanted to see in my neighborhood. This sign had power, said something meaningful. It projected the heart of a community. The signs in my neighborhood have purpose, yes, but they lack depth. They are superficial, more about daily existence and the self, and less about the collective soul of something bigger. So, as Sam and I turn east and head back home, I consider: *There must be more to the lives of those who live in these "little pink houses," more than their yard signs might suggest.*

Disheartened, I sit on a lawn chair in the backyard and toss a tennis ball for Sam. She returns it again and again until her tongue is long and her legs tired.

* * *

A few days after that trek past the neighborhood signs, on a new walk a few blocks from where we had been, Sam and I notice yet another placard, a brand new sign west of the main road, just over the border in the village of Westmont. A former church had been sold and renovated, and outside near the entrance is a large sign with a dark wooden frame.

The Madani Foundation

The old brick structure with big stained-glass windows is now the home of an Islamic center, standing in the middle of this traditionally Catholic neighborhood. The foundation's website says it's an educational institution to help Muslims and non-Muslims understand the true meaning of Islam through the teachings of *The Holy Quran* and the Prophet Muhammad.

Sam pays little attention to the sign when we pass it. Instead, she does what she always does when she walks the neighborhood—sniffs the trees, looks for squirrels, Prances when she sees another human nearby who might offer a pat on the head. Like the signs we saw days before, Sam cannot read this sign either. Still, I am certain she is heartened by a deeper comprehension. Sam did not see those signs in Oregon, the good ones or the awful, but I'm convinced, she knows what is a sign of hope. Despite the appearance of indifference, I am confident in her inherent sense of goodness. She knows that somewhere deep among the commonplace signs we witnessed on the hike the other day, and the symbols of hate Leslie and I saw in Oregon, there is innate *human* goodness. It's there. You just have to look for the signs.

Walk 11
The Visit

It had been weeks. Our schedules had never matched. But finally, after trying to make it work many times over, on a midday Monday, my son and I are able to get together. We meet at a dog park. He brings Franco, his golden doodle named after Franco Harris, the football great. I bring Sam, named after no one in particular.

Under tall blue skies and surrounded by the early leaf buds of spring, I begin with the matters at hand.

"Let me hit the marks," I say. "First, work?"

Graham gives me the ups and downs of his job, a warehouse worker at a large import-export company. It's pretty good going. But like all of us, he'd like a bit more understanding from the higher-ups about all the work he does. Graham is a good worker. He's strong and aware. And he has always had a propensity for thinking beyond himself, maybe too much, sometimes.

"Wedding plans?" I ask.

Graham is getting married next year. It's a long way off. But the venue has been chosen and he is ready to talk to photographers. There's not much to update because there's not much to do this far in advance. Still, I ask. Weddings bring high emotion. Asking questions is a way of unearthing those emotions, and maybe easing any oncoming anxiety.

"What about the search?"

Graham and his fiancée are living with his mom right now

but looking to move out, planning to find their own place. Buy or rent? Not sure. When is the move-out date? He's not certain.

The conversation shifts to the slumping Cubs, his brother's coming trip to Mexico to photograph a wedding, the detailed cleaning Graham is having done to his frequently messy car. And all the while, the dogs are off-leash, running hard, paws slashing through dirt and the gravelly trail. Franco, breathless and panting, chugs behind Sam as she gallops across the pathway, through strands of trees, and in between shrubs and wild bushes. Franco is older. Chunkier. Sam is lean and long, and joyful in this game of doggie tag. Graham, as we walk together, towers above me, big and bold. Even when he was a baby, he was still big in some way. He and his brother, two years older, were exactly the same weight and length when they were born, but Graham just appeared bigger from the start. His hair was longer; a tousled mop, darker than anyone else's in the family, almost black. When his mother and I would take him for walks in the stroller, people would think he was a girl—those long locks, those thick lips, that plump, soft skin. He grew up and out of most of that. Change comes to all of us. But yet all of us carry tiny bits of the characteristics of our earliest years. I guess I do, too. I think it might be my ears. And it's the same for the dogs. Franco had sleepy eyes. Still does. And Sam's hair might someday gray around her snout, but she will likely always be lean and long-legged and ready for a run.

The dogs are still zooming around. But suddenly they stop, both at the same time. They have noticed two other pups and the urge to investigate is strong. When dogs meet, initial strangers, they rush to go nose-to-nose, or nose or butt, as if there is something of much importance to discuss, to share, as if they have dire business to speak about, dog business.

The two dogs are with an older man in a blue T-shirt and shorts. He smiles and watches the exchange from a dozen yards away. One dog is a border collie with all of its patches of color and its nervous energy. It is less inclined to pounce toward the doggie conversation and stands aloof. But the other, a young one, caramel in color and smaller, apparently has much to say and trots toward Sam.

Hi. How are you? What are you doing? Do you like it here? Where you from? Do you like your owner?

Sam is tentative, but listens nonetheless.

"Franco," Graham says, "you going to say hello?"

Franco moves slowly, a few steps behind, his tongue hangs low and wet, and he's still huffing. He listens, too, to the caramel dog.

And you? What's up? Are you with her? Nice day, huh? Do you come to the park a lot? And your owner, do you like him?

The man gathers his dogs, smiles again, and walks on. The dogs follow, the caramel dog glancing over its shoulders.

See you again here, I hope. Enjoy the park. Have fun. Keep smiling!

Just ahead, a black and brown dog, sleek like a Doberman pinscher is chasing another smaller dog, nipping at the dog's side, snapping at its tail. The owner laughs.

"It's like the playground in middle school," Graham says. "Some kids are just little bastards."

Graham and I call for Sam and Franco to come close, and as we turn through a bend in the trail, we step more quickly, there in front of us is a dog only a cartoonist could create. It is slightly bigger than a healthy Chihuahua, one floppy misguided ear, and all white. Albino, maybe? There's pink around the outer edges of its eyes. And it's strutting toward us with fast, awkward feet that appear to be missing the point of their purpose.

"Oh my," I say, loud enough for the owner—a woman in her 30s, walking ahead of her dog with the leash in hand—to hear me. "It looks like a character in a Pixar movie!"

The woman laughs. "She's kind of goofy, I know."

Sam is busy sniffing a tree, but she hears my animated greeting and apparently fearful of missing out on something exciting, she hurries over. The dogs touch noses, stare at one another. Tails twitch. But this time, unlike the high-strung caramel-colored pup, this visit is more like a handshake at a cocktail party.

Nice to meet you, and what is it you do for a living?

And what is it these dogs do for a living?

Over the course of our walk, we meet more dogs. They say hello, play, sneer, and sometimes, but less often, ignore one another. They are like people at a party—looking each other over, sensing good energy or not, exchanging an uncomfortable smile. What is it that brings dogs together or shies them away from each other? In many ways, it is likely the same as with all of us—our own worth and sense of self, self-confidence, our moods, the chemistry, the things we have in common. And when Sam returns to this park someday, if she sees the same dogs, will she remember them and ask how things have been? Will she wonder about their jobs, their relationship with the fancy poodle down the street, will they discuss doggie treats, share dog food recipes, ask if they have summer vacations plans?

After the walk, Graham and I head to a pub where we sit on the patio and order a couple of sandwiches. We tether the dogs to our chairs. They slop water from stainless steel bowls the waitress has offered. Graham drinks water from a clear glass; I have a Smithwick's in a Guinness pint glass. We settle in, silent. Content. We have had our visit; we have had our say. There were no revelations. No surprises. Just being together, here and now, is all that matters. Father and son. As we grow older, these get-togethers are far less frequent and more cherished. Quiet and still, we sit, savoring the goodness of comfortable weariness. We need each other, still, despite that Graham is no longer a boy who must be looked after. And I—no longer the father who holds his son's hand when crossing the street or tucks him in at night—do not need to protect him from the world with unabated attention. Still, here we are, together, and it is exactly what we both want.

"Let's toast," I say, raising my beer glass. "To more days like this."

Our glasses clink and we drink.

The dogs are under the table on their bellies, their paws resting against each another, happy and satisfied. Their visit has been good, too, for they don't get together often either. When the world is off balance, as it frequently is, and the days pass slowly before another reunion, I will remember this.

Walk 12
Catch Me if You Can

I shouldn't do it. It's illegal, I believe. But I do it anyway. My wife says I'm a risk taker. I know I tend to push the envelope sometimes. But I love to see Sam run, the freedom she exudes, it's refreshing and makes me smile. So, I do it. I set her free.

Early morning. It is the best time for allowing Sam off the leash. Few people, if any are here at the park. And today, there is no one. Not yet. The ground is soaked. There had been a great deal of heavy rain recently and the small pond has overflowed onto the soccer field and the playground. I know Sam will run through it, and I know she'd be trashed when it is all over.

She bolts for the ducks in the now expanded pond, splashing her way through soaked ground, muddy water spraying up behind her. The ducks fly off and Sam stands elbow deep in the water watching them escape. She sees me on the asphalt trail and barrels toward me, runs past, stops, and quickly observes her surrounding, then zips off again toward a row of trees, rainwater puddled at the trunks. Sam slops and jumps and finds a stick. She carries it in her mouth, high and proud, and prances to the edge of the pond, water droplets flashing off her long ears.

For fifteen minutes, she romps. Happy, free, and soon tired. Her tongue is long. On the far side of the playground, I see an older woman with two beagles on two separate leads. She is watching me, watching Sam. It's an accusatory watch. She's judging me, this man with no leash on his wild dog. I call for Sam.

She turns to catch the sound of my voice, and then dismisses it for another run toward the ducks. I call again. She ignores me. Sam has done this before, so I do what I've done before. I start to walk away from her, up the walkway and toward the street. Sam has always followed, fearing, I assume, not being able to find me again. And, like before, she comes running. But when I reach out with the leash's hook, she freezes. Oh no, no, no. I'm not doing that, she is certainly saying. "Come on, Sam," I demand. "Let's go." Sam's eyes are wide and wild. She steps back to avoid my reach. "Damn it, Sam." I see the woman with the beagles, her eyes still on me; the criminal that I am. Sam runs toward the playground, up the hill, through several puddles, and then stops to watch me. I walk away again, fifty yards from her. Sam eyes me, waits for a moment, then gallops toward me and follows behind out of reach. "On the leash," I say, "right now." I think I hear her say, screw you. Yes, that's exactly what she is saying. What a defiant little bitch, I think. I'm mad, but yet, inside I am giggling. I don't want Sam to know this, of course. But, this cat-and-mouse game has become rather amusing, owner and dog, dancing around in the mud. Freedom—such a good thing, being carefree and limitless. Still, considering my own so-called risk taking, we all need a few boundaries in order to get along with the rest of the world.

I decide to stop trying to leash Sam and start to walk home along the sidewalk. She'll come, I say to myself, the little shit. Sam follows, yes, but again, just out of reach, a slow and methodical walk. I shake the lead in front of her nose, thinking she might try to catch it in her teeth and I can snatch her forward and grab her collar. But she's not falling for it. I keep walking, up the small hill to the other side of the street, one block and then two. I shake the leash again. Nothing. I call her with an angry voice and she stands back and stares. Maybe if I crouch to her level, eye to eye, appear less of an authority figure, she'll come close. I drop to the sidewalk, sit, and cross my legs. "Come here, girl," I coo. "Come on, it's all good." She stands at arm's length. Insubordinate. Calculated.

A half a block away, I see a woman standing near her home's driveway, watching me. She must be judging me, judging my dog, and my pet owner responsibilities, just like the lady in the park with the beagles. I got this, lady, I think. But of course, I don't.

"Did she get off the leash?" the woman calls out.

"Sort of," I say, standing now. "I let her off sometimes. She's usually good." I walk toward the woman, pretending to have things reasonably under control. "Maybe she'll come to you?"

The woman, smiling now, says, "Hello, cutie. Come on. Come on."

Sam watches the woman, but stands still. Sam knows what's up. I walk toward the woman and now see her dog—a big, boxy chocolate Labrador behind the nearby fence. The dog barks and Sam notices. This is it, I think.

"Ah," the woman says, "I think you've got it now."

Sam moves toward the fence to see her new friend and sticks her snout between the bars. "Gotcha!" I grab Sam's collar and yank her toward me. "You little shit."

The woman laughs. I laugh. Sam snorts. The great escape is over.

I snap the leash, thank the woman, and return to walking home. And while I grumble, Sam steps in silence, sullen but not sorry. I'm angry, but I wonder: *Am I not giving Sam enough freedom? Does she secretly long for it? And when a taste is permitted, does she find it so inviting that she would risk our relationship, risk my indignation?* It's silly to think this. Sam doesn't understand any of it. She just wants to run, to exhaust herself in the morning's cool air, to feel the celebration of splashing muddy earth. She only wants off-leash now and then. Just like all of us.

We are close to home now, a house or two away, and I unsnap Sam from her tether and watch her run through the yards to our home's front door. She stands at the stoop and waits. Sam is happy but tired. I am no longer mad. How can I be? How can I have mistaken ownership for freedom, obedience for love?

The answer is right in front of me.

Walk 13
The Life in Death

A couple of hours before sunset, my wife and I drive along a four-lane thoroughfare in our town. On the side of the road in a twisted heap is the body of a dead deer. It appears to be a doe, an adult, and, by the looks of it, it may have been there for several days. It's a grotesque sight, sad and disturbing. I grew up in Western Pennsylvania where seeing a dead deer on the road is not unusual. The population is plentiful in those hills and valleys, in the forests of pine and maple. Still, what is before us now—a lifeless animal with its eyes open and its contorted body—is distressing. At some point, a crew will come to take it away.

I have never buried a deer, but I've been a part of other burials—cats and dogs. As many as seven, if my count is correct, are under the dirt on the property of my boyhood home. My first dog, a collie given to me by my grandfather when I was just a few months old, is buried at the top of the hill in the front lawn where a towering evergreen once stood. Other dogs of my youth are buried in the backyard. Several near a rose bush, another under a maple. Cats here and there. Although I did not bury them, I most recently held the quivering paws and bodies of two dogs as they died on the floor of our kitchen, one passing away a year after the other. Age took both. I have the ashes of one in a square plastic container.

Death is on my mind as Sam and I step out for a quick

hike around the neighborhood on a Saturday afternoon. It is beautifully clear and cool. A perfect late spring day. So why think of death? I'm not sure. Maybe the dead deer made more of an impact than I know. For whatever reason, oddly enough, I am also thinking about my late sister. She came to me in a dream the other night, laughing after telling a joke about a truckload of penguins. I know the joke well; it was one of my father's favorites.

Guy is driving a truck full of penguins. The truck breaks down. He gives another guy with a different truck $20 to take the penguins to the zoo. Later, the first truck driver sees the second walking in front of a mall with all the penguins marching behind him. Hey buddy, he asks, I thought I told you to take these penguins to the zoo? I did, he answers. I had some money left over so I thought I'd take them to the movies.

In the dream, my sister is in full belly laugh. I am, too. We are both happy. The next day, in the light of the real world, I write a song about my sister, simple chords on a guitar. It comes to me in less than an hour. My sister died nearly two years ago. Sometimes death, its full significance, is not fully understood at first. It instead hides away, only to reveal itself at an unexpected time.

Sam and I head south and then east, and in my head I am singing the melody of my sister's song. It's good that it's there. And at the corner of the first cross street, on the concrete sidewalk, at a peculiar and strange time for such a sighting, I see another dead animal, a field mouse or maybe a mole. It's brown, almost black, and small enough to fit in a child's palm. Sam pulls me toward it and takes a quick sniff before I am able to pull her away. She is as curious about death as all of us, it seems. A predatory bird has not yet mangled the remains of this mouse or mole; its body shows no signs of a collision with a car or a child's bike. What killed it? Why is it here? I use a small branch that has fallen from a nearby tree and push its tiny body into the parkway grass, a less harsh place.

We walk north on the parallel street and Sam violently shakes her head, forceful enough to rattle the metal tags on her collar. It's a familiar shudder. She has been shaking her head regularly lately. My wife and I think it's something to do with her ears. So, I've been regularly cleaning them and using drops of medicine we received from the vet that is to help with a possible infection. It's a simple thing. Treatable. But on this day, probably because death is on the mind, I wonder if what is making Sam shake could be something more serious. *What a worrywart*, I say to myself. *Stop it.*

I tighten Sam's lead and scratch her back. "Don't have a brain tumor on me," I say.

Sam shakes again.

I ask her to sit. She does. And I lift one of her ears, slip an index finger inside and wiggle it around. Sam is tolerant of my poking and prodding. I find nothing. The ear is clean. I kneel to look closer. No redness or signs of irritation. Through it all, Sam remains still, her eyes shifting only slightly to see me.

We head farther north, then east, south, and west again. Surprisingly there are few people outside on such a sweet day. The sun is bright, there's a steady breeze. Sam steps proudly into it, young and alive. And all along our way, she never again shakes her head, and certainly never considers her curious condition, her ailment, and surely not thinking about her own death. For what does she really know of such things?

It's been said that one thinks of death more often as one ages. It's somehow hardwired. Natural. I guess I'm not so morbid after all. But Sam is just two years old. Fourteen in dog years. And like any teenager, she thinks only of her invincibility. Mortality is a ghost. Scientists say that in the final thirty seconds of life, we systematically fall away, first losing our sense of self, then our memories and language short out, until we are left with only a shell. But a most recent study suggests our brains actually know when we are dead. There's evidence that some brain waves are still at work several minutes after we are clinically gone. Still, death remains a mystery and a fascination for most of us. I wonder, though, what the dead are thinking today as Sam steps on. Are they watching us, smiling as we walk in the sun? As the poet Billy Collins wrote, are they looking down through the glass bottom boats of heaven? Is the dead mouse thanking us for moving its body to a more restful place? Is the dead deer calling out for dignity, for its body to be moved away from the violent rush of cars and rumbling trucks? Is my sister still telling her joke? And are all those dead dogs of my past insisting I get Sam to the vet to have her ears checked one more time? I wonder if it is not the point of life to sometimes think about death. For those who reflect on it most often, are they not more liberated from all the unimportant irritations of life, all the insignificant things we allow to overtake us? Once we understand death, don't we know better how to live?

I can see that Sam is happy to have shared the walk, as she always is, and happy now to be home, too. She's happy to be with me. She's happy to slurp the water from her bowl, happy to be offered a doggie treat, happy to get a scratch under her snout. There is certainly no way to ever know this, but maybe Sam's contentment is a sign that she knows a lot more about the end of life than any of us would ever have believed. And maybe by understanding it, accepting what will eventually be the inevitable end, we discover all we really have is now.

Walk 14
Rain

I awake to rain tapping lightly on the window behind the bed like the tip of someone's finger on the pane. It is a soft rain, misty and tender. It might be enough to delay a walk, yet it might be just right for one. I wonder if Sam hears it like I do, if she contemplates it like I do. She must know it's raining. But unlike me, she is probably not calculating how it might change our plans. For her, there must be a walk. It is inevitable regardless of the weather.

I clip Sam's leash and step out into the shadowy morning. There is a familiar smell—musty and earthy. Petrichor is what it's called. A couple of Australian scientists gave the smell of rain a name. The air on a rainy day is proven to be cleaner, fresher. The drops catch pollutants in the air, snatch bacteria and dander, and wash it away.

Sam raises her snout. She smells it, too.

The rain is vaporous and fine, and I consider going back inside for a hat, but dismiss the thought. Dubliners would not call this a rainy morning; the Irish would not even acknowledge it. Sam must be Irish. For her, it is only weather. It is what has been given us on this morning—nothing more, nothing less. Sam is aware of the drizzle, but she does not complain and instead embraces it, accepting it for what it is.

There is a pool of water near the walkway to the street. It must have rained all night. I step around it but Sam steps through it, the water to her elbows. I thought I saw her smile. We walk west and then south and for several blocks there is no one. Soon, a woman emerges from a cottage-like home with a garden for a front yard where droplets weigh down leaves and bend flowers. Her umbrella is red and it reminds me of watercolor paintings of lovers walking in Paris. Sam spots the woman and together we watch her move south at a hurried pace. I can see only the umbrella now, the hem of a dress, and the black of her shoes. And at the corner, there are two utility workers, wearing hardhats and yellow vests. They pause to watch her, too. It's a moment of joy in the drudgery. They are beginning the job of installing a new drainage line along the street. Mud is already on their jeans. Sam pulls me toward one of the men. She wants to say hello. But the man ignores us. The rain has dulled his spirit, it seems. I wonder if people believe they should be unhappy in the rain.

Sam is not unhappy. Her paws are soaked. The drizzle has dampened the hair on her back and head, and it hangs heavier now over her eyes. But there is a strut in her step, a bounce, as we move closer to the train crossing. Again, I think I see her smile.

Some dogs hate the rain. Won't go out in it. Not even to pee. Owners must pull them by their leashes into backyards and courtyards, the dogs vigorously resisting. They shake their paws in disgust when they reenter the home. It's a wretched event, but not for Sam. She knows one cannot sleepwalk through the rain. She knows how rain has a way of awakening something.

To the left at the street corner near the train is a village fountain. Two ducks sit in the water pool. In the parkway grass, a robin picks at the earth where worms come to the surface. In the mulch of a park's garden, mushrooms have appeared, growing in the damp and brief overnight hours, some shaped like tiny brown umbrellas and others like pink asparagus, each emerging from the shredded bark. The rain has aroused the living.

I tie Sam's leash around a bench outside the small coffee shop near the train station. Sam stands in the light drizzle and watches me through the door, greeting others who enter and exit.

"She's like a troll," says the breaded man sitting at the round table near the front of the shop. He eats a brown muffin and drinks coffee from a ceramic mug. "Protecting the bridge," he adds, smiling.

"And in the rain," I say. "Trolls like the rain, right?"

"You can't be angry with rain," the man says, sipping from his mug.

I buy a black coffee and a butterscotch muffin. The rain remains light, almost unnoticeable. We walk north on the main street and find another bench under the awning of a small antique shop. Traffic is picking up. A young woman walks by quickly, talking on her phone. "It's probably the rain," I hear her say to someone on the other end. I sit and open the white bag, pull off a small chunk of muffin, and feed it to Sam. She is wet around her mouth and I feel it on my fingers. I rub her long ears. They, too, are wet. She sits and I feed her another bite as rain falls on the tips of my shoes.

"This walk deserves a treat," I say.

But I wonder if the treat for her is less the muffin and more the rain. Sam has accepted the rain; she has not tried to find shelter. She has not ducked under the canopy of a tree. Even now she is on the wet side of the protective awning. I'm dry; she's catching the drizzle. And she is still smiling, as dogs smile. There is a reason kids jump in puddles, a reason for the joy. When we arrive home, I use an old towel to rub Sam's paws dry and pat the dampness away from her ears and tail, and I am reminded of children in the rain, and the wonderful smell of wet dog, oil and water merging, a scent that some find unpleasant, but not me, not today. For the musty perfume that surrounds me is the smell of happiness, of choice, of approval, and evidence of life.

Walk 15
Summer

The temperature had seared to 98-degrees. I didn't want to step out of the air conditioning and neither did Sam, but we both knew we needed to get out of the house. It had become an early summer's version of cabin fever, sizzling days forcing the world to stay inside. How many more emails could I read, Facebook posts could I reply to? I had finished two books. I had rearranged my clothes closet. And Sam was restless. She had found socks from the hamper and had held one of them in her mouth for hours. She had taken shoes from our closets and shirts from the basement laundry room and had brought them to the first floor. Bored while the world outside soaked itself in sweat.

"Once around the block," I say to Sam. "We can do this."

We step out the back door into a wall of dense, heavy air. Sam usually jumps from the stoop to the walkway, but not today. She moves slowly, purposely, as if being slowed by the shear thickness of things.

"Come on," I say, leading her through the gate to the driveway and out to the front yard.

A reminder here: Sam is a black dog with curly, thick hair. It must be unbearable.

I tell myself not to complain. Not to moan about the weather. Enjoy that it wasn't a day in January. But as we round the first corner, I am already sweating and Sam is panting. Even the flowers planted along the edge of a neighbor's property appear to be wilting.

I slow my pace and allow Sam more time to sniff and meander in the parkway.

Why do people move to South Florida or Arizona and 110-degree heat? Those I know who live there tell me the heat, unlike the Chicago cold, does not keep them from going outside. As I watch Sam slump around the corner and I feel the unrelenting sun on my neck, I'm not sure I agree with that assessment. These temperatures would keep a desert lizard inside an air-conditioned home. These same people tell me it's easier to acclimate to the heat of the south or southwest than to a Midwest winter, but I'm not buying it.

Sam and I walk north now. I wipe sweat from my forehead. Sam looks up at me. Can we go home now?

Up ahead, I hear voices, children talking, laughing. Standing in the driveway of a small home on the east side of the street, a woman holds a garden hose by her side. A young boy and girl stand near.

"You want to run through it?" the woman asks, squirting the hose at the children's bare feet.

The kids dance to avoid the spray, appearing tentative, unsure.

The woman squirts the hose again, inches from them. "Come on," she encourages. "It's fun."

My father used to set up a garden sprinkler in our yard when I was a kid. My sister and I and a few neighbor friends would put on our ill-fitting bathing suits and run back and forth through the cold water, over and over, for hours. Does anyone run through a sprinkler anymore? This woman with the hose in her hand, who may be about fifty years of age, must have a similar memory. And she wants the young children, most likely her grandchildren, to find the joy in the simple act of cold water on bare skin in the heat of a summer day.

The two kids are still not yet ready for the spraying water, not certain of this generations-old activity. It must appear foreign to them, prohibitive.

"With our clothes on?" the boy asks, smiling.

"Sure. Why not?" the woman says.

You can spray it my way, I think. Put it on streaming and squirt this old man and his dog. Soak us!

The boy and girl look at each other, as if hoping to find courage in togetherness. The boy giggles. The girl giggles. The woman aims the hose over their heads and offers a quick squirt, water droplets fall on the children and they scatter to escape. The woman laughs and aims the hose directly at them, the steam chasing the kids as they dart across the driveway to the lawn, attempting to outrun the attack, their high-pitched screams carrying down the street.

All of this has Sam's undivided attention. She's alert and seems to have forgotten about the heat. The laughter, the joy of summer, has won her over. Even in the insufferable intensity of a June day, there is happiness. Stretching the lead toward the sounds of children, Sam is now aware of only them, of their delight, of the woman's playfulness.

We turn at the north corner and head west and south again toward home. The hum of a window air conditioning unit cuts through the nearly impenetrable air. With the children behind us and out of sight, the cooling unit's purr is the only sound I hear. Even the birds do not chirp. It's as if Mother Nature has thrown a heavy hot blanket over the neighborhood, numbing the signs of life. Sam falls back into tired steps, her head hanging low, and I wipe accumulated perspiration from the back of my neck and brow; the sting of salty sweat forces me to close an eye.

Only a few minutes ago two children and one black dog found an oasis in the sun. For a tiny piece of an afternoon, the pall of a merciless day vanished. And although the walk was one we had not looked forward to and had the makings of a miserable memory, it had reminded me that summertime, like childhood, does not last forever. The sweet burn of the sun is to be celebrated for what it is—the opposite of winter—a season in which to surrender.

Walk 16
Sam, the Buddhist

It is an odd thing, a woman and a man walking, not side-by-side, but apart, together but separately. He is in front, marching at a particular pace. And she, ten steps behind, hunched and scuttling, as if trying to catch up yet purposely keeping a distance. Are they together or apart? This is the second time I've seen this couple. The first was from my window at the dinner table the other night. Now, it is Sam and me who see them on a sunny Sunday and we are nearly crossing their path.

"It's strange," I whisper to Sam.

Our hike around the neighborhood this late morning has been peaceful and quiet, the kind of walk where you are keenly aware of your strides, your easy pace. But now Sam is out of rhythm as she pauses to watch this couple, this peculiar pair, walking in some offbeat ritual of obedience.

Maybe I am being judgmental. What do I know of them? Maybe he is simply a faster walker. Maybe he takes longer strides. Maybe her legs are short. Maybe she has a bad knee. Maybe he was once a daily jogger, a track star in his younger days, and can't help himself.

"They're like Mormons," I whisper to Sam as the couple takes the crosswalk at the corner.

That's likely not a proper comparison. I'm simply thinking about cultures where men take the superior role, where women are dutiful, submissive. To be fair, that's not true of all denominations within the Mormon Church, only the ultra-patriarchal systems of the fundamentalists. Still, it comes to mind.

The man is dressed in jeans, a red golf shirt, and white sneakers. She has long hair pulled back in a ponytail. Her shorts are navy blue; her loose-fitting top is sleeveless. She, too, wears white sneakers. Neither would ever stand out for any other reason than this odd straight-in-line, purposeful, almost ceremonial walk. They speak no words. They do not acknowledge one another. We watch them, follow them, for over two blocks and there are no smiles, communicative gestures, and no deviations from the steady pace. This is not a walk for pleasure. It can't be. This is a walk for another reason, a walk to prove something, to gain something, to feel accomplishment, to feel worthy, to feel somehow better about themselves.

The Buddhist monk, Thich Nhat Hanh speaks of meditative walking, pilgrim meditation, he calls it, and how in this style of travel we are always *arriving*, our home is in the present moment. I like to think, although it is not easy, that my walks with Sam are in this tradition. The goal is to be keenly cognizant of your stride, and to smile, even if it is forced, as it is believed that you will be happy if you act happy. I try to do that in some fashion most days. I think Sam does, too. By traveling this way, you are honoring the Earth, the monk tells us, for it is what balances your steps. Enjoy yourself, he tutors, and use the time to reacquaint yourself with yourself.

I wonder if this couple has ever considered this.

There's a quote I love from the writer and teacher, Paulo Coelho, the author of *The Pilgrimage*, his account of his walk along the road to Santiago in Spain. It comes from the pages of a subsequent book, but it could easily have been taken from text of The Pilgrimage:

"Walk neither faster nor slower than your own soul. Because it is your soul that will teach you the usefulness of each step you take."

I wonder if this couple knows of Paulo Coelho.

Sam and I stand at the corner where the couple had crossed and we see them now march up the slightly elevated sidewalk. He remains in the lead. She behind. And I remain intrigued by this walk of un-togetherness. But then I wonder: Do they recognize or respect or even consider the purity of a good walk? The couple appears to be on a mission, a militaristic hike with a less than mystical goal. Theirs is not a pilgrimage. When I walk—with or without Sam—I am only occasionally successful in meeting the mindfulness I set out to discover. It comes only in miniature spurts, little moments. But Sam, she is different. Sam is always in the present. She is always putting paws to pavement and honoring the ground she walks on, enjoying herself through the art of a good walk. Her sniffs, her prances, her total awareness are in each step. She is better at this than I, than any of us, and apparently far better than the couple we've been observing. Sam is a natural. She gets it, understands walking's essential spirit. Like it must have been for our human ancestors hundreds of years before cars, trains, planes, and buses, Sam knows how to walk. And although much of those earlier human walks were utilitarian—simply a reason to move from point A to point B with a focus on destination—walking was also considered a pastime, a way to socialize, to unwind, to rediscover the unhurried world. Sam does this every day. She does not need to get from point A to B to find food, to catch a commuter train, or pick up the mail at the end of a long driveway. Why does she want to walk as much as she can? It makes her happy. Why do I walk Sam? It makes *me* happy.

Sam and I step south from the corner as the couple treks over the crest of the hill and disappears. Sam quickly forgets them and their detached, unchanging gait, for she is now tugging toward the large elm tree in the parkway where she can catch a scent at its base and return to her pilgrim's walk, the one the

Buddhist monk talks about, a monk about which Sam knows nothing, a monk whose philosophies Sam will never study or contemplate. But this is of no matter because Sam is a far more natural traveler of the world, the most mindful monk I know, a teacher of the perfect way to move in the world.

Walk 17
Shoeless

If there had been a conversation with anyone who would have seen the two of us walking this morning, it might have gone like this:

Excuse me. Do you need help?

No. Why?

You're barefoot.

Okay?

Do you need shoes?

No. I have plenty at home.

Then you're not homeless?

No. Not homeless.

Doesn't it hurt?

Not really.

Hmmm. Okay then. Sure you don't need help?

No thanks. All good.

The questioner would then have gone home to tell his partner, maybe the boss at work, and friends at the next outdoor deck party about the strange guy walking his dog around the neighborhood, wearing nothing on his feet.

This didn't happen this way. No one talked to Sam and me on this walk. But you can imagine how it could have played out this way. You see, you can talk to yourself, blare the radio from your car, text while driving, carry a gun in a holster on your visible hip and apparently none of this is as crazy as walking barefoot down a suburban street.

I had read a recent news article online about the beauties of walking barefoot and thought, why not. So, Sam and I head out before the weather turns hot. It is supposed to be steamy later. We want to give this barefoot adventure a try before the pavement heats up. In the article, the author wrote about how natural it is to walk this way. How barefooting promotes good sleep, helps with immune system activity, reduces stress. Medical studies even suggest walking barefoot prevents disease. And although barefooting is not what most of us do, Sam does it all the time.

I take off my shoes just inside the front door and hook up Sam's leash, and the two of us, naked from the ankles down, head out to touch skin to earth.

Sam jumps the last step of the stoop. Her paws land on the concrete and she walks forward without a wince or reaction of any kind. I, on the other hand, recoil from the ground's stark coolness. It is not that I haven't walked outside without shoes before. I've gone out for the mail and the newspaper at the end of the driveway, walked barefoot around the house to water the gardens, but this morning, I am more aware of the sensations. So when Sam and I move to the sidewalk in front of the house, there is a noticeable sting. The concrete here is less smooth, grainier than the walkway near the stoop. I pull Sam to my side and try walking on the grassy parkway where morning dampness tickles the balls of my feet. On concrete or grass, I walk slower than I have on other walks, something Sam is not fond of. I'm tentative. She's not.

Sam looks at me as if to ask, are you okay?

"Give me some time," I say.

I continue walking the parkway as we move around the corner, but the ground soon becomes uneven and I return to the sidewalk. After a few steps, my brain seems to adjust, lowers the volume of the sensory signals and any tenderness I had experienced just a few minutes before quickly subsides. My mind accepts the sensations. Sam, on the other hand, needs no time to adapt, of course. Her feet are made for this. Her pads give cushioning to protect the bones and joints from the shock of walking and running on any surface. The pads are also insulation against the weather, damp grass, and even the rough concrete sidewalk. She pulls me forward, trying to pick up the pace. But I pull her back. With these naked feet, slow is better for me.

I catch a small rock on the heel.

"Damn," I grumble.

Sam turns her head to me.

"It's nothing, Sam. Just human frailty."

This will not be a long walk for my feet are unprepared for a lengthy trek. This is clearly not the barefoot of a soft sandy beach. I feel exposed and self-conscious. But I step on, knowing that this kind of walking is not as unusual as one might think, it is even historic.

In the late 1800s, mailmen walked barefoot along a stretch of the Florida coast between Lake Worth and Key Biscayne Bay to deliver packages and letters. At the time there were few roads even though settlers had claimed land in the area. Soon there were enough people to warrant the U.S. Postal Service to extend mail delivery. But the only way to do it was to employ mailmen who would walk the sixty miles along the beaches. Not the manicured beaches of today's resorts. These were rugged, uneven, even washed out. The barefoot mailmen became legendary. Sam Snead, the great golfer, learned to play the game barefoot in the backcountry of West Virginia. He was too poor to afford shoes. Snead said if there had been tournaments where everyone had to play barefoot, he would have won them all. And at the Olympics in Rome in 1960, African runner Abebe Bikila of Ethiopia ran with the marathon over the hot streets in his bare feet. He took the gold medal in a world-record 2:15:16.2.

About halfway through our walk, Sam stops to pee. While she does her business, I check the bottoms of my feet. There is dirt and a few minor grass stains. The callous on my left big toe is inflamed, but only slightly. I brush away tiny pellets of debris that have collected on the outside of my right heel. Walking this way now feels doable. I've adapted. There is oneness with the ground.

"Sit, girl," I tell Sam.

Sam lowers her butt to the grass then hesitates half way into the movement as if wondering what I'm up to.

"Go ahead."

She does.

"Paw."

Sam offers the left front.

"Good girl."

I twist her leg to see the pads. They are black and scuffed in spots. They are rough like medium gauge sandpaper.

"See mine," I say, lifting the bottom of my foot to Sam's eye level.

Sam looks at me, then my foot, and then licks my heel.

"Why, thank you, Sam," I say.

Her tongue moves to the ball of my foot and then my toes.

Veterinarians have told me that dogs lick because it's pleasurable. A salty taste is nice and a lick or two releases endorphins. But dogs lick for other reasons, too, more instinctive reasons. Mothers lick their puppies to clean them and pack members will lick to communicate. It can be a way for a dog to welcome another as a member of the tribe. The dog being licked does not reciprocate, instead stands tall and takes it, accepting the invitation to be part of the pack.

Could it be that Sam's licks are her way of welcoming my attempts at a barefoot walk? Are her licks a kind of knighting, like a queen resting a sword on a shoulder?

"Thank you, Sam," I say again as she licks my arch.

We have just under a block to go before reaching home and as we turn south at the corner, I see a man in his driveway about to enter his auto. He wishes us good morning but says nothing else. He sees my bare feet, I'm certain. But the conversation I had imagined does not happen. The man is certainly secretly judging, he must be. But what he doesn't know about this odd man, wiggling his toes in every crack of the neighborhood's concrete sidewalks, is this man's attempt to be like his dog. Sam understands what's going on here. Sam knows what I'm doing and why, this rookie member of the society of barefoot beasts, a member initiated by licks, encouraged by a wagging tail, and one worthy of stepping out again someday with not a single thing on my feet.

Walk 18
America

It is early morning on the Fourth of July and Sam is wearing a red, white, and blue scarf, a cloth bandana with images of nautical flags tied around her neck. It's a touch of the holiday from the groomer. I never liked those silly scarves, but it's Independence Day, so I tolerate it. Still, it feels like forced patriotism.

We walk a quiet neighborhood. No one is outside in the first couple of blocks. But signs of The Fourth are everywhere—red, white, and blue door ribbons at a front entrance to one home, small American flags line the walkway of another, a child's bike rests in a yard with the spokes of its wheels laced with crepe paper in American colors. One would sense a bit of pride running through these streets, pride in country, pride in the American way (whatever that is) despite the rat's nest we are in—trade wars with China, a war of words with North Korea, deep questions about immigration, and a president with zero class, no empathy, and questionable ethics.

"What is it we are celebrating here, Sam?" I ask.

Sam sniffs some day lilies along the parkway on the street near the railroad tracks.

We head east and the neighborhood begins to come alive—a runner, a couple of early dog walkers, and several adults on bikes, one after another. This is not the usual morning crowd; these are the holiday people, the ones taking advantage of the day off to head outdoors before breakfast, before firecrackers snap, charcoal burns, and the town's parade steps off.

I stop at the corner and look at Sam. That stupid scarf. I untie it, remove it, and tuck it in my pocket. Sam does not protest.

It's an odd relationship I have with this holiday. I love my country, even though I'm not sure what that really means. I believe patriotism also means pointing out what needs work, what needs attention, what we do wrong and maybe how to change it. I scowl at nationalism, the sightless admiration of a country just because it's your country. I was never in the military. Missed the mandatory draft. Wouldn't have gone to Vietnam if called on, instead I would have left on a bus to Montreal. And my father, who was a veteran of the Korean War, told me he would have bought the ticket. My relationship with America is complicated.

"Sam," I think aloud, "would you fight for your country?"

Dogs have a long history of being in warfare. In ancient times, dogs were scouts. The Egyptians, Greeks, and Persians used them as sentries and patrols. George Washington, who would later be named the Commander and Chief of the Continental Army, brought his favorite dog—Sweet Lips—with him when he attended the First Continental Congress in 1774. It makes sense. Dogs are so keenly loyal, a trait necessary for military service. The animals in the pack survive because members of the group depend on each other, not unlike a military unit, a squadron, a platoon.

Still, despite my complex feelings about this country, its military hubris and its tendency to forget history, it is hard on this day not to feel something good about America. It remains a shining light for many, despite its imperfections. After all, the day is not meant to be about military service but rather a celebration of an incredible idea—American democracy, even if it is flawed, flawed when the Founding Fathers gathered in Philadelphia and flawed today. Flawed like all of us, like our heroes, our families, our lovers, our friends, and even our dogs. And, on the matter of whether Sam would fight for the country—she wouldn't, unless I trained her to do so. Like humans, dogs are not natural fighters. Their instinct, like ours is to want to bond. If a dog is a fighter, it's been conditioned to be that way by a human being, who, for whatever reason, believes the animal must be aggressive, combative. Dogs, like us, don't want to fight. They want to love and be loved. I like to think *that* instinct is more linked to the idea of America than warfare. Even though we fought bloody battles for our independence, what makes us a virtuous country is our ability to want to bond, to be empathetic. America is like Sam. It wants to love and be loved, and to accomplish this, it doesn't need to blindly wave its flag or wear a silly red, white, and blue scarf around the necks of its dogs.

Walking north now toward home, I see a small dog, a terrier of some type, sniffing around a garage door. It is untethered, free and roaming. The dog sees us, Sam and me, and scampers closer. Sam notices and pulls on her leash. She does not bark or growl, instead there is simple interest. Who is this dog? We slow down and the dog follows, its tiny tail raised and twitching. "Hello," I say. The dog ignores my greeting and rushes to Sam. The two dogs sniff each other. And from over my shoulder I hear, "Can you grab him?"

A woman walks barefoot from two houses south, carrying a small leash.

"He got out the back door," she says.

I reach to corral the dog, but it darts into a yard a few feet away. Sam pulls toward it and blocks the dog in between a large bush and a tree, as if to keep it from dashing off. Sam then stands close to the dog, her long legs on either side of it, obstructing its movement.

"Thank you," the woman says to me. "And thank you," she adds, nodding toward Sam.

"Almost looks like Sam knows what she's doing," I laugh.

"Oh I think she knows," the woman says and reaches to pat

Sam's head. "She was trying to be helpful," she adds in baby talk.

I'm not ready to give Sam that much credit, but it would be nice to think she truly had been trying to help, that she cared about the little dog's safety, about the woman and her worries that the dog might be too hard to catch. It would be lovely to think Sam had been showing compassion; that her instincts were for good, that community was on her mind. It would be wonderful to believe that Sam may understand the whole of us, what really matters. America's educational system is in a sorry state. We imprison too many people, our healthcare system is an inequitable mess, too many of us own too many weapons, we are chums with authoritarian leaders we should ostracize, racism runs through us like gangrene. But, what we have above it all is collective empathy. I believe that.

After thanking us again, the woman leashes her dog, and as she walks back home, she calls to us, "Happy Fourth!"

Sam and I head to our back yard and I toss around a tennis ball she has left in the lawn. It is far too early for fireworks, it's not time to light the grill, and the band members in the parade have not yet gathered to play Sousa's "Stars and Stripes Forever," but Independence Day is here, and one can trust that the idea of America might still be alive, that its people and its dogs might still believe this lofty experiment has a chance.

Walk 19
Alone Together

It's an inventive idea, taking the black strap from an old piece of luggage in the basement and tethering the two dogs together. Leslie and I had agreed to watch my son's dog for the weekend as he and his fiancée headed off to a family lake house in New York State, but Graham forgot to bring a leash. So, if I wanted to walk Sam and Franco together on one lead, I would have to be creative. I connect the old strap to the two dogs and Sam's leash to the strap. It is ingenuity at its best, a true MacGyver-ism.

Franco, an ivory colored golden doodle, is clearly the alpha, always tugging on his lead toward something. Sam drags behind, the luggage strap stretched out and taut. We move north along our street and immediately the strap tangles around Franco's front right leg. He begins to hobble, continuing to wrench forward. Sam's head is yanked downward, her collar spraining her neck. She scampers forward to relieve the pressure and snarls the leash around the trunk of a small tree and my left ankle. We are only 500-feet from the front entrance of our home, been walking for only three minutes, and I realize my invention is a bust.

Walking two dogs at the same time is a skill that requires far more patience than I have. I consider giving it up entirely, but instead, release myself from the entrapment, readjust the strap, shorten the leash, and try again, wrangling with two anxious, excited K-9s who, by no fault of their own, lack the discipline and grace to fall into any Clydesdale-like rhythm.

Is it even natural to walk two dogs at the same time? Are dogs meant to be hitched together? Dogs are social beings, and yes, they crave the pack dynamic. But as Franco, Sam, and I take the curve in the street and the dogs nearly knot the leash and themselves around a small garden fence, I am certain they sense my elevated irritation.

A couple in the neighborhood walks their two dogs most evenings, but they do it as an independent team. He takes the older one on one lead. She has the other on another. Unconnected. Unattached. They walk them in the middle of the street, to allow for room to keep distance between the two dogs so they can tug when they want. It seems to work. I think about this couple when Franco, once again, somehow gets the strap caught up around his leg.

There are double doggie leashes. They're sold at pet shops. The straps are tethered with a mechanism that allows for swiveling, lessening the chance of tangling. But I don't have that now. Wishing does me no good. At least Sam and Franco are of similar height. Sam weighs about 40 pounds. Franco is only a bit bigger. They have similar energy levels. It's not like I'm walking an elderly English sheepdog alongside a hyper, nervous teenage Chihuahua. Still, I had hoped this would be a far easier task.

I shorten the walk for reasons of sanity, taking the parallel street and heading south, a shorter route home. There are more tugs, more tangles, mostly the minor variety, but we keep moving. Halfway down one street, despite Franco pulling on the lead, Sam decides to abruptly stop. Her legs stiffen and she refuses to move. Franco jerks back against the stretched-out leash and appears annoyed. Sam looks at me. She clearly has had enough. She wants to be unhinged. *Can't I just do this by myself? Can't I do this alone?*

We hear so much about separation anxiety and how healthy dogs are social dogs. But, like us, don't they, too, need their own space? Some *me* time? Solitude? Wouldn't Sam love some time to be walking the neighborhood by herself, in isolation, without Franco, surely, but also without the leash or without me? Being alone can recharge us, help us rediscover ourselves, find independence and escape the grind. Still, psychologists say many people would rather take an electric shock to the head than sit in a room alone with their thoughts. No wonder solitary confinement is a form of punishment. But learning to accept aloneness can be healthy. Solitude is a higher consciousness. Embrace it and it can be a wonder. But Sam is not looking for a higher consciousness right now. She simply wants relief from this disagreeable tandem.

At the front stoop to the house, I disconnect the makeshift double leash and Franco dashes inside. Sam begins to follow but hesitates at the threshold. She eyes me, making sure I am right with her, that I am also coming inside the house, and that we'll all be together, unleashed, in our pack, with the family, alone together.

Walk 20
Dog Years

It is the weekend of our annual Cubs holiday. Each summer, my sons and I attend two games at Wrigley, just the three of us. Casey comes in from his adopted home of Seattle and joins his brother and me for a Saturday-Sunday series. One game is already in the books—a loss, sorry to say—but Sunday's is in front of us. And I'm up early, before anyone else, walking Sam around the block.

We first started attending Cubs games together, my sons and I, when they were young boys. They played T-Ball and Little League and found baseball likeable, not a passion, but reasonably fun. It seems so few kids feel the same way anymore. Baseball is no longer a fast enough sport.

Since the beginning of this mini love affair with the game and attending Wrigley, several dogs have passed through our lives—Hogan, Mike, Cody, and Franco—their childhood Wheaton terrier, their boyhood Labrador, Casey's dog, Graham's dog, generations of baseball alongside generations of dogs. Time marked by America's pastime and puppies, boyhood to men. Sam is part of that timeline, the youngest of the markers. As usual, her girlish energy pulls me along the sidewalk. There's a bounce in her pace. But there is no such bounce for me. I'm feeling my age—tired legs, achy back. Yesterday was a long day. We returned home at midnight after the game, fueling ourselves through nine innings with mustard-covered hotdogs, break-the-shell peanuts, and plenty of beer. Indulgence, routinely administered by the young, has clearly worn out the old. I'm hoping the walk with Sam will regenerate an aging man.

I'm reminded that the boys are men, too, as Sam tows me towards the trunk of a towering maple in the parkway so she can sniff its base. Graham will be married in the spring; he's buying his first house. Casey is settled in Seattle—home, friends, dog. He, too, is considering a new home in his city, a new venue closer to his work. Growing up. Grown up. Older. And how old, I wonder, is this maple tree Sam is now sniffing? How many rings would it show if we sliced it open? Some say trees talk to each other—this maple may be in conversation with the oak and the smaller maple just a house away, the roots exchanging thoughts about soil, water, sunshine, and maybe, the ills of aging. Trees talking about dead branches, about old peeling bark, about how dogs sniffing at their trunks is annoying, no longer cute as it once was in their younger days.

Change, it has been said, is the price we pay for becoming. And we become through days, weeks, and years of engagement—the boys and their father, the boys and their dogs, Sam and me, even Sam and the trees. These are not our only encounters, of course, but they are a chapter in the ongoing exchange. And they lead us to our true selves. In part, Sam is who she is because of the walks with me. I am who I am, partly, because of my walks with her. The boys are who they are, in some tiny way, because of our years of baseball weekends.

Sam and I cut through the edge of a neighbor's yard and I notice how curious she is about this home's front door. She watches it as we move, eyes locked on the doorway, the alertness of youth. *What's over there?* I wonder. Another dog, I presume, one just on the other side of the entranceway, out of sight. Another encounter, one she won't have today, but one she wishes for. And as she ages, will this impulse, this urge to connect still be there? When Sam no longer yanks on her leash with excitement, no longer chases the tennis ball, when she no longer paces with anticipation before our walks, will that be the end of her becoming? I wonder, too, if that is true for me. Will age and its inevitabilities dampen my need for meaningful encounters or change how I feel about weekends like this one? I hope not. I hope never. Pablo Picasso said, "Don't waste your youth by growing up." But, at some point, we don't have a choice, do we? The attitude, the zest, the exuberance for a life of youngness is ratcheted back, not by our own battle against the timeline, but instead because it is life's design. Age is a thief. It steals pieces of us.

We turn at the crossroad to head home and Sam is showing no signs today of ever growing old. There is only ebullient youth. Pure. Authentic. Her walk is the walk of a teenager—one of spirited abandon. A week ago Sam turned two years old, an adolescent in dog years, but maturing is not on her mind. Like all teenagers, she believes only in immortality. And maybe, on most days this is what we should all believe in, that life is forever, that time does not alter us, that aging is nothing more than hands on a clock, that we should believe in living forever, that we will never grow old or creak our way through a morning-after walk, and that the boys and I will always have our weekends with the Cubs even when they have to wheel me up the ramp to the centerfield bleachers.

Sam and I are back home after the quick trek around the block. We move slowly through the rear door. The house is still. No one is awake. The morning light is low and soft between the window blinds. Sam lifts herself to the living room's leather chair and curls in, paws crossed, head on the chair's arm. She is satisfied and sinks into the quiet of the morning. I take the seat next to her. I, too, ease toward the peace of daybreak and watch the empty street through the window, believing that this welcome stillness after an early walk has served us both well, will serve us well through our separate days, and maybe somehow, has allowed a bit of Sam's youth to rub off on me and on the rest of the world.

Walk 21
Iowa City

The posters are everywhere. On the window at the front door of Graze, a restaurant in Iowa City's trendy section of downtown. There's another on the door at Cortado, a coffee shop. Two more are tacked to the wall in the entranceway of a Chinese restaurant and on a bulletin board inside Prairie Lights, the renowned bookstore. The search has been on for more than a week for the missing University of Iowa student. Mollie Tibbetts went out for an evening run near her home in Brooklyn, a farming town, where she was staying with her long-time boyfriend and has not been heard from since.

We are in Iowa City with Sam. Leslie and I have agreed to stay at the home of her daughter and boyfriend to water the houseplants while they're away on a tour of South Africa, a long-awaited trip. Sam is here, too. Sam likes Iowa City as much as we do. The college town has an artsy, literary vibe, and the home of the Iowa Writers' Workshop. And it was in this town that Leslie reclaimed her life, living here for two years to reevaluate after a divorce and a successful, miraculous battle with cancer. She is alive when she should be dead. Plus, her daughter and son were attending the University of Iowa when she moved here. It was a good place to settle in, learn to crew on the Iowa River, do yoga, walk her then dog, Dakota twice a day, and rehab an old English cottage close to campus. It was her personal sabbatical. As for Sam, she's been to Iowa City before and she is happy to be back.

How do I know this? It's her strut, the canter she has when I walk her here—different, somehow, than back home.

Leslie and I decide to have lunch and a coffee before heading back to the house and then out again to a friend's home for homemade Indian food. This is when we first notice the posters. In the middle of each is a photo of the young girl. She looks so happy. But it is gloom that has overtaken Iowa City, even as the town prepares to host 20,000 guests for RAGBRAI, the big bicycle ride across Iowa. Mollie Tibbetts did not go missing here, but she was part of this town. She was a member of its tribe. She walked these streets.

After lunch, we drive back to the house, and before heading out for dinner, I take Sam for a walk. We move along Melrose Avenue away from campus in bright late afternoon sun. Sam is alert, taking in new smells, watching a robin hop across a lawn. She knows she is on vacation, it seems, enjoying the freshness of a getaway. We turn left on Sunset Street and there, nailed to a maple a tree, is a different poster. It's the announcement of a missing cat, a tabby named Leo. The poster tells us that Leo is friendly and knows his name. There's a phone number and an address. A reward is being offered—"a good amount of money involved"—it reads.

"Someone is missing their friend," I say to Sam, pointing to the poster. Sam looks at me longingly, as if to say how sad it is to hear of a missing pet. Sam has never been missing, but she's certainly has run too far from me in the park, a defiant adolescent testing her boundaries.

It is so trivial—this poster of a missing cat after seeing the dozens of signs downtown of the missing university student. No one can compare the two, of course, but they have similarities. Both are signs of human struggle, unbearable worry—certainly of widely differing degrees—but on the same spectrum. They are both dramatic shifts in life's unpredictable narrative. One moment all is well; another your world is turned upside down—

happiness to awful dread. It can also go the other way, of course, terrible to wonderful. Both of these stories could, I pray, have happy endings. The cat will come home; the girl will be found. Alive and safe.

"Maybe we can find the cat on our walk, Sam," I say. "Keep an eye out, okay?"

Sam looks at the poster and then sniffs the trunk of the tree on which it is tacked. I wonder if she's trying to find Leo's scent.

"And maybe," I say, "we can keep an eye out for Mollie, too."

Change is inevitable. It is an obvious statement, isn't it? But I think we are reminded of this most when our hearts break, when life makes the days difficult or, for the family of Mollie Tibbetts, unimaginably agonizing, a desperate anxiety that is inconceivable. Certainly not all change is bad. Change can be renewal, reaffirming, or restorative. Babies are born. Marriage. Old friendships renewed. And these changes, no matter the kind, do not happen alone. Loved ones, friends, even our pets are symbols of change.

Farther along on Sunset, Sam and I hear voices, the sound of children playing. On our left just over a slight hill, a playground comes into view. Mothers and kids are gathered near a swing set, a seesaw, and a small water fountain. A dog, maybe a Shetland sheepdog mix is running through the spraying water while a little boy chases it. One of the mothers smiles at Sam. I smile back.

Sam was *my* change. She was *our* change, Leslie and I. She came to us in a rather unconventional way. Sam had been the pet, a young pup, to Leslie's first husband, but his girlfriend was allergic. Leslie's daughter brokered a deal and we took Sam in for a weekend, a sort of test drive. We fell in love.

Before Sam's arrival, however, there was a period of sorrow. When Leslie and I moved in together, before our marriage, we each had a dog. Leslie had rescued Dakota, a Chow-retriever mix. The dog had been abused, left chained outside. Remarkably, he was a gentle dog, but he had a snarly attitude sometimes, one cultivated by enduring those tough early years. Dakota had a way of giving you the finger; he didn't seem to always care for people. But then he would cuddle up to you and pine for a hug and a scratch, and fast become your best friend. My dog was Mike, short for Michelle, a female yellow Labrador with all the usual attributes—unwavering friendship, a perpetual smile, and the kind of lack of intelligence that breeds untiring joy. Mike was everyone's buddy. She loved everything and anyone who came within licking distance.

Mike died first. She had been ill, throwing up ugly bile. The vet suspected the worst. Maybe kidney failure and suggested it might not be very long. Leslie and I were scheduled to be at an event for the Ernest Hemingway Foundation of Oak Park just outside Chicago and had been reluctant to attend, knowing Mike's condition. But we thought maybe just a few hours would be okay, so we blocked her off in the kitchen with a baby gate, left her plenty of water, and planned to come home early. When we returned, Mike was lying in the same spot where we had left her, the water bowl still full. Her tail thumped the wooden floor when we entered the house.

That night, sometime in the wee hours after we had gone to bed, Leslie was shaken from her sleep by a metronomic click and a scratch. Les touched me on the arm and whispered. "Do you hear that?" I lifted my head from the pillow. "Oh my," I said. "That's Mike."

Mike had remained in the kitchen, in the same spot and position, the baby gate in place, and she was now extending her front right leg to paw at the floor, a rhythmic signal. *I need you. Please come.* I am certain, absolutely sure, she was calling for me. I knelt on the floor and put my arm around her chest, patting her head as her breathing became labored and halting. I held her until the end.

A few months later, Dakota began to struggle. Age had

caught up with him. He had become disoriented. We would find him staring at the wall. He would lose his balance and fall down. Leslie found it too hard to be with him in his final hour. Again, I spent a night on the kitchen floor, holding another dog until its last breath.

Leslie didn't want to take possession of Dakota's ashes, but she did keep his collar. I, however, have Mike's ashes. I'm not sure why I felt the need to keep them, but I did. Someday I'll find the right place to scatter the remains.

Months after Dakota had died, Sam came into our world. Leslie admits she wasn't as ready as I was. I had been secretly researching rescue dogs, breeds, looking at photos of agonizingly cute and forlorn pups at the animal shelter. Then we had the two days with Sam, the trial run, and we were smitten. We made the arrangements, were given Sam's toys and leash, and offered to allow Leslie's ex to visit and walk Sam anytime. But we also made it clear, as hard as it was, that Sam was now in a new home and she was ours. There were no givebacks, no returns. Sam could not be taken away. We saw her as our change, our commitment, our new beginning. Mike had been my dog; Dakota had been Leslie's. Sam was ours.

Dogs can't speak for themselves. Their only advocate is you. They have no say in who will take them on, so it is up to us to keep Sam healthy, make her happy, defend her, shape her growth, and help her flourish. I'm still trying to find out what's the best way to do that. I've had dogs most of my life, but these have always been tough questions to answer. How do you balance master and friend? It's more than feeding her grain-free dog food to keep away the allergies that force her to scratch her ears. But undeniably one of the ways is to walk her, offering her the world, essential for her and me.

My regular walks with Sam began at a time of change for me. I had turned 60 years old, had become more sedentary than I would care to admit, gained a few pounds, lost some zip. Sam was a puppy, just a year old when we brought her into our house. It would have been unfair, irresponsible to be a couch potato. It was imperative that I exercise her, the perfect remedy for an aging man. Sam is helping me walk into a new decade with a new outlook, to face a time of natural decline with a renewed assurance and belief in the restorative power of walking, of caring for another living thing, one looking to you, and only you, for nearly everything she needs and wants.

We are still walking the streets of Iowa City and our hike has taken us to West Benton Street, a busier avenue. We turn left past ugly brick and stucco apartments. I have my phone with me and check *Google Maps* for the best return route. The app suggests another left, but when we make it the road only leads to a construction site and a newly carved dirt street. New condos are being erected here and Google has no idea the roads that were once here have been bulldozed. Maneuvering through tall piles of earth, stacks of stone and bricks, Sam and I take a narrow unpaved road on the edge of the construction zone. There's a large crane truck working along a strand of trees just to our right. Sam pays no attention, but I do. In an effort to make more room for the condos to come, the operator guides the big crane toward a tall and majestic tree, first smashing the crane into the high part of its trunk then backing up and colliding with the lower section. The big tree teeters, wobbles, defying the hefty effort to take it down. The operator slams into the tree again and the tree gives up, snaps and crashes into surrounding trees, ripping branches away, its towering trunk dropping, seemingly in slow motion to the brush below, creating the disturbing sounds of collision and destruction. Sam jumps, lets out a mild yelp, and snaps her head toward the crash. She's quivering now, leaning into me, startled by something she has never heard before, never seen.

"It's okay, girl," I say, kneeling to hug her neck. "It's just the sound of men working. Development, you know?"

Sam sits and moves closer to me.

"Maybe not progress," I continue, "but definitely change."

Sam stands; I loosen her leash, and lead her to the paved road just ahead. We make our way to George Street and the app gives us a better, more reliable route to follow. At Highland Drive, a few yards in front of us, attached to a utility pole, is another poster of Mollie Tibbetts. My chest aches. I am not sure there is a god, but I say a little prayer anyway for Mollie, another for her family, her boyfriend, for everyone who has ever known her. I say a prayer for Iowa City. Difficult times like these are not noted on our Google calendars. Instead they sneak up like ghouls in the night. What we can be certain of is change. Good or bad, tragic or miraculous. We can only hope we will know how to find our way through it.

As Sam and I near the driveway of the house where we are staying, I see a blackbird on the roof. He's cawing at something. It is not a cry of distress or fright. Instead there is something sweet in the sound, something fresh to sing about, some new change for the bird—new hatchlings born to the world, maybe a new nest to crow about. Sam stops and looks up. She watches the bird as it takes flight and follows it through the air. As it passes just overhead, Sam leans on her back paws and lifts herself to the sky as if to greet it somehow, as if to say, I'm with you, birdie. I'm with you.

Walk 22
The Beauty of Bacon

There is no walk for Sam this morning until she gets it right.

It is 6:10 a.m. We are in the backyard and it's a standoff. I am adamant and Sam is defiant. Although I'm not sure she knows it. Her attitude is rebellious. *I'm not going to do anything just because you say so. In fact, I'm most likely not going to do it at all, simply because you asked.* This is what I'm dealing with as I hold bacon in my outstretched hand.

"Come," I say firmly, holding out a sliver of the salty, meaty treat.

Sam stares at me.

"Come," I say, again.

She does not move.

Sam is a good dog. She's a *great* dog. There have only been two issues: her itchy, troublesome ears, and an occasional, extremely annoying stubborn streak. There was the time she and I were at the park and she refused to come directly to me, lingering behind, just out of reach. What I'm facing this morning is a part of that maddening personality trait. She's too damn smart. She has learned that when I call "come" that may mean Leslie and I are about to leave the house without her, or she has to give up something she likes—a romp at the park, meeting another dog, getting her nose in the garbage, or what I'm facing this morning, ending her sniff-fest around the backyard.

"Okay then," I grumble, "you're not getting a treat."

Earlier this morning I fried up some bacon, let it cool, and placed the strips in a plastic baggy. It's been suggested to up the ante on the treats when you're trying to train a dog. And whatever it is you are attempting to get them to do, only give them that certain premium treat when they perform that particular request. So, when Sam comes to me on my command without hesitation, when she comes directly in front of me, pauses to look at me, then, and only then, will she get the bacon.

I sit on one of the metal lawn chairs, trying to appear less like I'm going to scold her.

Again, I offer the bacon.

"Come."

Sam is ten feet away and not moving.

"Come."

Sam takes one hesitant step toward me.

"Good girl," I purr.

Sam takes another step.

"Oh, good girl," I say, wiggling the bacon, believing twitching meat is somehow more appealing.

Sam is closer now but standing still, again. Progress has halted. So, I slowly stand to offer the bacon at closer range, thinking maybe Sam just needs to get a better whiff. This turns out to be a bad move. Sam reacts by stiffening and hopping back two steps. It's a playful, catch-me-if-you-can move, the same thing she does when she sees me with her ratty tennis ball in my hand, preparing to watch it fly. She wants no part of my bacon-fueled plan.

"Come on, Sam," I moan.

Sam offers a mischievous growl and a sharp bark.

"No," I snap. "It's too early for that."

She barks again, falling into what might be best described as a three-point-stance. Another bark, another hop, another rascally growl, the catch-me-if-you-can dance, and another woof.

Behind me I hear the bedroom window slide open.

"Can you train her some other time?" Leslie's comment is formed in the style of a question, but this is not a request. "It's too early," she pleads.

"I can't keep her from barking," I say.

"Later, please? The neighbors."

I look at Sam. *Damn it.*

I thought I could do this work in the quiet of the early morning when Sam would have little distraction and focus only on me and the bacon rather than neighbors, other dogs, or some squirrel scurrying around the trees.

I am wrong.

I walk behind the garage. "No walk until you come," I say. Sam follows and together we are out of sight of the bedroom window and the back entrance. Sam stands ten feet away. I hold out the bacon.

"Come."

Sam stares.

I drop the hand holding the bacon. "Really?"

Sam does not move. No expression. Poker-faced.

"Jesus," I'm bellyaching now and move past her toward the back door. "No walk then," I mutter.

Sam stands still, only her head moving to follow me.

I step to the stoop and stop. *One more shot?* I turn, offer the bacon, and give a little smile, hoping a shift in attitude might do it.

"Come."

Sam is fifteen yards away near the back of the garage and facing me now.

"Come."

She takes a step.

"Good girl."

Another.

"Good girl, Sam."

She stops and slumps her head, taking another deliberate

step, and another. Sam is now three feet away.

"Come."

She is suspect, but she is almost there.

"Good girl."

Inches away, she looks at me. She looks at the bacon. Again, she looks at me … slowly lowers her butt … and sits.

"There you go! Good girl, Sam!" I kneel to her level and give her the bacon. She takes it with great care; maybe a bit unsure she deserves it. I put my hands on either side of her head and vigorously rub her ears. "Good come, Sam! Good girl!" Her leash is in my hand now and I shake it. "Walk time!" Her ears perk up, her eyes brighten, and her tail wags. I clip the leash to the collar and offer a hardy rub of her back. "Good girl." Sam pulls toward the gate, and with the small plastic bag of bacon strips in my pocket, we begin.

One loop around the neighborhood is a good reward, I figure. And as we step off it appears all is right with the world. Crazy Guy, who I've written about before, has resumed his chalk art on his driveway. It's what we all expect. *Super CFL* is written in big bold letters. It's a reference to the famous radio station WCFL of the 1970s. His front door is open and I consider, if only for a second, walking up to say hello. But then I'm reminded it's only 6:45 a.m. Still, I'm pleased to have thought of it. A few houses down the block, the big old and deaf golden retriever is slumped on the lawn of its home, its head in its front paws, eyes closed, motionless, as always. And around the bend, on the north side of our street, the yard of the house with the young couple and the three little kids looks like the ransacked warehouse of a former Toys "R" Us. I smile. It is proof that all is well, all is constant, all is as it should be.

It occurs to me now that this sameness—Crazy Guy, the old dog, the neighbor's yard full of toys—this "habit" of the neighborhood is what I am trying to break in Sam. Her "habit" is to continue the catch-me-if-you-can game when I call her. It is what I have come to know. It is Sam being Sam. And now I want to change her. I want to break the "habit." *It's for her own good*, I think. *It's a safety thing, ultimately. It's important for her to listen to me, come when called.* Change is forever and inevitable; it comes when we are not looking for it, out of the shadows. We lose a job — our spouse asks for a divorce. A friend dies suddenly — we win the lottery. Anticipated change or sudden change, but it is still change, nonetheless. Training a dog to obey a command is of minor consequence in the great scheme, but change is not. This new "habit" I'm trying to form in Sam is a change.

We are a few houses from home and I want to give it another try, one more time to re-enforce the behavior. I drop Sam's leash. "Stay," I say. She sits and I walk a few feet in front of her. "Stay," I repeat.

I reach for the plastic bag in my pocket and pull out some crispy meat. "Stay," I say one more time. I wiggle the bacon and Sam is quick to notice.

"Come," I command.

Sam puts her head down and walks directly to me, sits, and looks into my eyes.

"Good girl!"

She accepts the bacon. I rub her ears.

Back home inside the kitchen, I go for the trifecta.

"Come."

There is no hesitation. She comes right to me. I kiss her on the top of head and slip her another strip.

It's still quite early and Leslie remains under the covers. She stirs when I move quietly into the bedroom.

"Hi," I whisper. "I think Sam's getting it."

"Okay," Leslie whispers back.

"And when you go to the store today," I add, "buy a big slab of cheap bacon. We're going to need it."

Walk 23
Of Parents and Children

The doe stands six feet tall in knee-high brush just off the trail. Its eyes follow me like a cop. Sam watches the doe, silently but intently. The deer ignores her; Sam is of no matter. It is only me she studies.

"How beautiful you are," I whisper, my eyes on hers, unwavering.

I notice the fawns, one just beyond her and another farther back. Her babies are light brown with faint white spots dotted on their bodies, like Bambi. They're too busy munching on sapling leaves to see us. And that is why the mother is not about to blink; for she would do anything she has to, anything she must.

It's 6 a.m. We have been in this section of Fullersburg Woods, a county forest preserve, for only a few minutes, walking past the old stone lodge built during the Depression on the loop trail along the banks of Salt Creek. The morning birdsong has only begun and the creek is high but hushed in its movement, its current only noticeable when it ripples across a fallen tree branch. I have come here for quiet, Sam and I, early in the day when the parking lot and the trails are empty. There is much solitude, peace only the woods can give.

I am out of sorts, today. It's a number of things—a chronic stomach issue is flaring making it uncomfortable to sleep, but more importantly my younger son has been unexpectedly blue despite coming to a final deal on a new home, a place to begin a life with his fiancée, and despite the anticipation of a trip to see family out east who will hold a wedding shower for them. Instead, it seems, things are stressful. This so-called "adulting" can be daunting. There is much to do, much to plan for a big move, for a wedding—paperwork, and lenders and lawyers. It's not overwhelming for most, but it is a lot for him, a young man finding his way. I feel a bit silly worrying about it. Still, it's there. Stress is a sneaky thing.

Sam and I step slowly along the trail and the big doe keeps her eyes locked on me. Sam remains alert to the deer, but does not pull on the leash. There is no growl or huff. It's a little curious, her behavior. Sam has never been this close to a deer before and it's as if she is hushed by its presence.

"What do you think girl?" I quietly ask. Sam snaps her head to me in response. But quickly returns her attention to the deer.

The doe steps closer, a move I do not expect. She then lifts her left leg in an exaggerated manner and aggressively stamps her hoof on the ground. In the quiet of the early morning, there is a distinct thud. She does it again. The deer's eyes do not waiver. Thud. *What is this?* I think. I learn later that a deer will stamp its hoof when it senses possible danger. And a doe may do it as a signal, a call to her young that Momma is a little worried.

I am amazed how Sam is taking this. She does not see the stamping as some measure of hostility. Maybe Sam knows. Maybe she understands. Sam is not a mother, she has been spayed, but instinct is a powerful thing. Maybe Sam does not react to the deer's parental signal in the manner I would expect because she comprehends the concern. Maybe when Sam was a puppy, her mother snapped at an aggressive dog who came too close to the litter, or maybe she understood her mother's menacing soft growl when a fox paced the fence of the Indiana farm where Sam was born.

I hope to telephone my son later today. Help where I can. Ease some anxiety. Maybe my stomach issues are related, my own worry surfacing. But I also question this thought. Parents want to protect their young, save them from the unpleasant, wrestle away the threats. It's only natural. It's instinct, like the doe. But there will be a time when Momma won't be there to stamp her hoof and the children will have to figure it out on their own. Life in the woods can be scary. But it can be beautiful, too. Look at what I am witnessing in the early light of this day, the majesty of it. The beauty, however, is only realized on our own terms, with our own eyes, our own hearts. Beauty, security, serenity come to us only when we decide to let them.

Sam and I watch as the mother turns and ducks into the woods. The fawns follow. They do not run. They are safe. They are certain of their place here. The doe has determined that we are not a threat; we are not here to harm. We, too, are out to welcome the day, embrace the quiet, and find a little harmony.

At a junction on the trail there are wooden signs marking the way and I think of taking another path, but decide to stay on the loop, only to realize our half-an-hour walk has been one big circle. I laugh. "Look familiar, Sam?" I ask. The old tree trunk bench at the creek's edge we had seen earlier is again in front of us. I take a seat, pull out a handful of cooked bacon slices from a bag in my pocket and feed them to Sam. She sits to eat. This is when I hear a now familiar sound. Thud. Directly across the trail, fewer than twenty-five feet from us is the doe, the same one, her eyes on me, and again she stamps her hoof.

"Doesn't she know who we are?" I ask. "Remember us? We're cool. No worries." Thud. "It's okay, Mom," Thud.

Just behind the doe are the fawns. The mother shields them now, creating a bodily barrier. Soon, the doe backs up and slowly steps through a strand of maple trees, the fawns shadowing her, and all are soon out of view.

I offer Sam more bacon. "What kind of parent would you have been, Sam?" I ask. "As good as her?" Sam chews; her dark eyes blink. There's a glint from the low morning sun. "I think I know the answer," I say and scratch her head.

I will hold off calling my son. I'll be right here if he needs me. He knows that. And as we leave the preserve's parking lot, I roll down the car's windows and Sam stretches into the breeze, her eyes on the woods, watching, one might believe, for the doe and her babies, hopeful that everything is all right.

Walk 24
Back to the Garden

Sam knows nothing of Richie Havens' frenetic acoustic strumming, Country Joe McDonald's "Gimme an F!" chant, or Hendrix's electrified "Star-Spangled Banner." She knows nothing of the bad "brown acid" or how a festival with an unexpected mass of 500,000 people ran out of food and how the miles and miles of standstill traffic closed the New York State Thruway. But Sam does know mud. Woodstock celebrated mud.

Our walk today is on the anniversary of Woodstock and before heading out Sam has been sloshing around in our backyard where several days of rain have created a sloppy mess. She is not quite the naked teenager on that dairy farm in New York State, but, like many of them, Sam has been reveling in the muck. Her paws are caked. Her belly is brown from wet splashing dirt. There is no sense in cleaning her up, not now.

I hook the leash and head to the sidewalk.

Woodstock is all around me today—on the radio, in the newspaper, listed on my "Morning Briefing" email from the *New York Times*. It's been decades since Woodstock. How can that be? I was 12 years old in the summer of August 1969. I knew there was something going on. The festival, with all those the crazy kids was being played out on TV with Walter Cronkite, the nightly news my parents never missed. But it didn't register. Even though I owned a Sly and the Family Stone album and a Creedence Clearwater Revival record, the idea of going to a

115

concert hundreds of miles from my home in Pennsylvania to see these bands and others, attending any rock concert of any kind, was not yet part of my life. This would come years later, of course. I did, however, buy the Woodstock album that was released nearly a year later, played it until the grooves hissed from wear, listening to it with my eyes closed, dreaming how it might have been.

Sam knows nothing of this dream, not until today when I tell her all about it.

"If I had been a few years older, Sam, I would have been there," I tell Sam as she sniffs the dirt mound in the parkway just around the bend from the house where crews have been working on new drainage ditches. "Got in a car with a bunch of friends and started driving," I continue. "And that big pile of dirt you're admiring? That would have been a hill of sloppy mud. You would have slid down it while Joe Cocker belted in the distance."

There's freedom in dirt. Those kids at Woodstock believed in the recklessness of play, of making things better in the mess of it all. When it rained and rained some more, the freaks let it fly, they turned the mud into face paint and muck into joy. Sam is only sniffing her little hill of dirt, but yet she's fascinated by the raw grunginess of it. I wait her out, let her take in what she has discovered. She paws at it and sniffs some more. Sam does not know Woodstock, but it is in her spirit.

We head east and then north, and from Crazy Guy's house I hear music coming from an open upstairs window.

"That's Canned Heat, Sam," I say.

A radio station is remembering the day with music.

"Goin' up the country," I sing, "baby, don't you wanna go?"

We remember the songs. They still resonate, much of the music remaining not nostalgic but forever embedded in so many songs that came and still come afterward.

Sam looks toward the house and the window, she's curious,

but I'm not sure why. Is it the music? Is it the volume? Either way, Sam dances a bit when she hears it.

"Yeah, it does make you want to move," I say.

So many have come to know Woodstock as a cliché, as some hippie monument from "back in the day." That's sad. Too often those who see little more than tie-dyed shirts and stoned teenagers diminish its significance. The true story of Woodstock is much bigger, much deeper. Yes, it was a mess—poor planning, endless rain, all those people invading a small rural town. But it also was a generational benchmark, a vision of something better.

"There were hardly any arrests, Sam. All those people, and no violence." That is mostly, if not entirely true, and all with little security. A few cops, ones who could get through the traffic disaster were there. But not enough to truly do anything if real trouble had broken out. The gigantic crowd, in essence, policed itself. The Woodstockers shared food, fresh clothes, shelter from the awful weather, and drugs. "Peace and music for three days, Sam," I say, feeling self-conscious for a second after repeating a romanticized quote from one of the many overly sentimentalized online stories that have surfaced in the last few days about that weekend at Max Yasgur's farm.

"But yet," I tell Sam. "We just couldn't keep all that goodness going."

Woodstock turned out to be a lightning strike, a utopian flash. The *real* Woodstock could not have been anticipated. It was the perfect counterculture storm. It was magical, yes, but unsustainable. That kind of spirit has a short shelf life, a sad reality of the human condition. The beauty of Woodstock was not to be prolonged after that wet weekend in August of 1969. The ugliness of the era soon resurfaced—the war raged, Watergate was not far away, and the world's rotten side, what remained then, remains today, hiding under the shaky spirit of a touchstone moment. In some ways the ugliness is not hiding at all. It is out in the open, staring back at us.

Sam and I stand at the crossroads. Our walk has turned out longer than what we had anticipated. I take a breath and think.

"Let's go a little bit more, Sam," I say. "Let's make it last. Woodstock deserves at least one more block."

Sam's ears perk up. Maybe she understands. We cross the street, turn right and take the next road to head south for another half-a-mile or so. And over the tops of the houses more than a block from the open window at Crazy Guy's house, I think I hear Joni Mitchell's "Woodstock." *We are stardust. We are golden.* Or maybe I just *want* to hear it; I long to hear it. Maybe it is not there at all. Maybe that's me singing those words to myself, in my own head, just for me.

Walk 25
In the Eyes

Sam is quite the creature, certainly unlike most dogs I know, maybe unlike any animal I know—a sleek body built for running, long elegant legs, and those astonishing eyes, big and round; the black irises and the porcelain white sclera. And those coal black eyelashes, long and elegant, delicately curling upward, as if tempting you to touch them. When Sam is alerted to something, the lashes twitch, acting like the farmer's forked tree branch, the dowsing stick, signaling some inescapable discovery.

On this evening it is squirrels.

The tree climbers are everywhere along our walk tonight. Rabbits, too. The temperature has dipped, humidity is down, so maybe that's the reason they are bustling about—scurrying up trees, ducking in and out of hedges, hopping over curbs to dash across the street. It's the season. Late August. Fall is close. It's time for creatures to prepare. It's time to get back to work.

I've also returned to work. The sabbatical is over and the college calls. I'm okay with that. I've had a productive and restorative stretch—a book has been released, an audio book complete, a new manuscript sold, I've written some music, something I haven't done in a long time. Students will be back in the classroom in two weeks, and so, like the squirrels, I'll be scurrying soon, too.

I had been at the college all day today and Sam and I now need some time together. An evening walk will do me good, as my stomach again has been touchy with off and on grumbling and mild queasiness. I told the doctor that sometimes walking helps. He still wants to do a colonoscopy, so there's that. Also, Leslie and I had been dog sitting Franco, my son's dog, for a few days. Sam now needs some singular attention and I would like to believe she missed me today. When I came home, she rushed to the door, carrying in her jaw a red rubber toy bone, a gift for my return.

Sam and I step off in our usual direction, south to the corner and east, and it is at the turn that we first notice the squirrels and rabbits—one after another, pairs of them, sometimes. I wonder what Sam sees and thinks. She, like all dogs, hears and smells more than I ever will. What is it that truly interests her here, the squirrels or dreams of chasing one? But is that all she thinks about? She's an intelligent dog, she must consider more than this. Does Sam have desires bigger than squirrels? Does she have aspirations? What are they? Does Sam have dreams beyond the obvious?

I'm reading the book *Rising Tide Falling Star* by Philip Hoare. Hoare is an angel of the sea. He lives it, swims in it every day off the coast of Cape Cod or his hometown of Southampton. He communes with the ocean. I understand that urge. When I was a boy, I wanted to be an oceanographer. All those Jacques Cousteau shows on television captivated me. It was my dream to do what Cousteau did. When I was a young man, I visited Woods Hole and the Oceanographic Institution and fell more profoundly in love with deep waters. Somewhere that dream faded. New dreams took over. Has Sam ever had such hopes, such dreams? Does she want to *be somebody*? Does she know Rin Tin Tin, Lassie, Lady from *Lady and the Tramp*? Does she want to be Marley, Air Bud, a pampered pet from *Best in Show*? Or does she live only in the present, only in the now, all those squirrels her only concern?

In a tall maple tree two squirrels sit together in the crux of dual branches just above our heads. Sam watches. She doesn't bark. Doesn't lunge toward them. But her ears lift and those lashes twitch. The squirrels have her full attention. It is a remarkable act, really. Such keen alertness, a level I might never quite understand. It may be one of the reasons dogs fascinate me so much, their ability to be so single-minded at a precise moment. And when they focus on us, the master and friend, it is extraordinary.

There was a time when humans worshipped dogs like gods. The Egyptians loved their cats, but dogs had a sacred role in religious art and tradition. The Aztec peoples had burial sites for their dogs. The dog is part of Chinese astrology. And when the patron saint of dogs in the Catholic Church, Saint Rocco caught the plague, as the story goes, and went to the forest to die, it was there that he befriended a stray dog that licked his sores and brought him food. Saint Rocco lived. And to this day in Bolivia, Christians celebrate Saint Rocco and the so-called birthday of dogs on August 16 of each year. Saint Francis of Assisi tamed a wolf, the dog's ancestor, because he believed, like the human, that it was a creature of God. It is not unreasonable to think dogs were put here for a reason.

It is a lovely night to walk. The angle of the evening sun gives the late day a deeper color; the refracted light is more agile, more alive. The large locust tree in the parkway soars higher, the pink azalea in the big pot at the doorstep shimmers; the white lilies along a shaded walkway are more delicate. English ivy clings to the gray bricks of the home near the corner; the greenest growth climbing the highest. The giant evergreen in the yard permits the blue sky to filter through its branches, as if it is sharing its needles with heaven.

Does Sam see any of this? Is she using her amazing attentiveness to notice the beauty?

Sam is more interested in other matters—tugging on the leash to stop me, seeing another squirrel, this one scampering under a large leafy bush between homes. I watch Sam closely. Those eyes, darting, aware, and expressive. These are human characteristics, of course, but I see them in Sam. I'm interpreting her expression, something many of us do with our dogs. We see the sad face, the happy one; we see fear or anxiousness. Scientists in Finland recently found that humans are just as good at interpreting a dog's face as we are another person's. This doesn't mean, however, that we can put ourselves in our pet's place like we can with fellow humans. In Sam's case, I can't truly understand her interest in squirrels over the beauty of the evening light, but I might be able to tell how she feels. And maybe *that* is the real reason why dogs are here with us, to share something together, pure and real, beyond the complicated emotions of a human relationship. What does Sam truly see with those eyes of hers? And what do *I* see in those eyes of hers, below those glorious lashes? Maybe we see the same thing. Maybe Sam is admiring the evening as much as I am, just in a much simpler and authentic way, even when a squirrel snatches her attention. Maybe the answers are in those eyes.

At the last turn home, on the opposite street corner, there's a man walking a little dog, a scrappy thing with wiry gray hair. The two take a short cut across the street. The man and I smile, catching one another's eyes. I don't know what the man sees in mine, but in his I see comfortable weariness. He, too, I imagine, has had a full day, and like me, he walks his dog to come down from the day's buzz. And the dogs, they pull toward each other. We allow them to sniff noses and they, too, look briefly into each other's eyes, Sam's lashes twitch, and the two of them share something beyond squirrels, beyond what mere humans might ever know.

Walk 26
Aloneness

It is 5:35 a.m., and I sit in the brown leather chair in the living room in the dark. Only a small book light allows me to see the pages of *Summer*, the last of the seasonal series by Knausgård. Leslie calls Karl Ove my "man crush." I devoured his unlikely literary phenomenon, the thirty-six-hundred-page autobiographical novel, *My Struggle*, and now I'm sinking myself into the final installment of his unusual essay series marked by the times of the year. This morning, he writes of his aloneness and his comfort in it. I sit with only Sam at my feet, alone by human standards. She is motionless, her head between her outstretched legs on the hardwood floor. I'm aware she is there; aware she needs to go outside soon. But it is too early and I worry about the skunks. We have many in the neighborhood and they tend to show themselves in the dim light of the early morning. So instead of tending to Sam, I read. And I wonder if Sam likes the aloneness, too. Although, in a dog's world is resting at the feet of its master, even in this silent dark morning, truly considered alone time? We hear so much about dogs being social animals, animals of the pack, I still wonder if being alone is ever a dog's desire.

I have always liked being alone. I've fantasized about living singularly in a remote cabin, filling my days with walks and writing. Thoreau did it. But as we all know, Walden was just a short walk from town. It wasn't exactly a hermit's retreat. But yet

Thoreau found solitude there. And I guess that's all that counts. I've built my own "cabin in the woods" by erecting a shed in the corner of our home's yard where I can work and write alone. It is filled with books and art, and it is my alone place. My love of aloneness is not to say I am anti-social or don't love my wife or my children, or have some hidden need to be reclusive, or that I am some depressed misanthrope plotting some awful crime. It's only that aloneness is part of who I am and I embrace it. This moment in the dark with a book and only Sam at my side is a silent joy.

Time passes. More light filters through the window, muted a bit by clouds. I hear Leslie stir, hear her enter the bathroom, and Sam lifts her head to the movement. It's the first sign of a level of restlessness. "I should get you out, girl," I say, closing the book. Sam stands on all fours and turns to look at me. She knows. I put on shoes, grab the leash from the hook near the rear door, tuck a plastic bag in the hem of my pocket-less shorts, and take the steps to the rear walkway. It is still gloomy and a nearly unnoticeable drizzle continues. Still, I decide to go without a hat, without an umbrella. I like the idea of this.

Overnight storms have left a mess, a level of minor destruction. Small tree limbs litter the yard and front walkway. I pick up one about the size of my arm and toss it to the street. I kick another, a small one, to the curb. Long puddles have formed in the low spots of the sidewalk. Sam walks through one and then another. It is quiet out here. No cars. No people. The heavy grayness gives me the feeling of hiding under bed covers, a sense of retreating from something, another level of aloneness.

Does Sam feel this? Or is she looking about, sniffing around for someone, some other animal, to bring her company? She's with me and I sense the happiness she shows when she is out on a walk, but does her pack mentality call for more company than me? Like a human wanting more than one friend, longing for a big family, does Sam need more?

We turn north at the corner, and I find it curious that I hear no birds this morning. It is as if the weather has sent them away. Where have they gone? Are they hiding in their nests alone? Or are they together with other birds, huddled, finding shelter in each other? This is the difference between alone and lonely, I presume, the difference between giving yourself to others and the solitude that allows you to come back to yourself. I suppose Sam and I are experiencing a little bit of both.

Walk 27
September

September is made for poetry and song. It is a melancholy month, tender in many ways, a time for beginnings and endings—the start of new school days and the end of summer's promises.

There are shadows of September in the face of a young girl waiting at the corner a block from my home. I'm guessing she's fifteen years old, her long hair pulled back in a simple ponytail, her long legs holding up a gangly body and a slightly hunched back, stressed by the weight of an over-stuffed red backpack. She is alone, looking to the distance, apparently anticipating a school bus, as the first days of the school semester have come. If she is aware of Sam and me, she is not about to acknowledge this. Disinterest or painful self-consciousness has its grip. Sadness surrounds her, but yet she is somehow hopeful, as if waiting for something, a fresh experience more beautiful than what has come before.

Earlier this morning, I sensed the same longing in Sam and me. I have headed back to school, not unlike the girl, and classes at the college are underway. But my sense of longing has nothing to do with this return; it is instead about a departure. It started from a dream, still there when I awoke. I'm standing on the stern of a boat, watching the shoreline disappear as I head out to sea. I am missing someone, yearning for them. I don't know why, don't know who it is, but the feeling is profound. Sam, on the other hand, longs for attention. It was evident in the way she had come to my bedside, the way she had used her paws like human hands to wrap around my arm and pull on me, as if she could no longer delay the day, as if she, too, wanted to hurry and stand at the corner with the girl. I rose from the bed, pulled on some old shorts and a black T-shirt, and grabbed my phone and earbuds. I rarely listen to music on our walks but the September mood had taken hold—poetry and song—and so, I clicked on a *Spotify* playlist I had made years before, one entitled "September," and stepped into the coolness of the morning, Amos Lee's "El Camino" playing in my ears, Sam by my side, and there at the first turn, the young girl, waiting.

Some say "El Camino" is a song about Johnny Cash, a tribute of sorts. Others say it is Lee's ode to parenthood, his own maybe, or a letter to a new love. But to me, it has always been about the longing for some new awareness and finding the courage to embrace it, a song just right for this morning, this new month, for me, for Sam, and maybe for the girl at the corner. I want to say good morning to her, but she appears far too vulnerable. So, I pull Sam's leash close and walk by with no words, only the lyrics of Lee's perfect song playing in my head.

Sam and I head north, and one after the other the songs come. Glen Hansard's "Winning Streak," is encouragement for a friend, a lover, a child. It reminds me of Bob Dylan's lullaby to his son, "Forever Young." Jason Isbell's "Cover Me Up," is about getting sober and finding a new love. "She Treats Me Well" is Ben Howard's song of contentment. In Joni Mitchell's "Chinese Café" she embraces age, and forgives herself for giving her daughter up for adoption so many years ago.

Sam and I continue north toward the three-way intersection. To my left, there's a man on a front porch, typing away on his laptop, a mug of coffee balancing on the wooden railing. On the side porch of another home, a couple sits together in quiet conversation. The junk man's truck rumbles past, the payload unbalanced and teetering, the driver heading for the streets two blocks east where fresh throwaways line the curb. Garden workers unload an oversized lawn mower from the back of a red flatbed truck, and up ahead, a large shorthaired dog rests in a driveway, attentively watching our approach.

"You see him, Sam?" I ask. Sam is keen to the dog. The two are now locked in a stare.

In my ears I hear Bruce Cockburn's "Going to the Country."

Sam snivels along the base of a tree in the parkway at the corner as an older woman with silver-white hair and pink tennis shoes appears from the west. She smiles at Sam and then me, waves, and walks to the street to avoid us. The woman is on a pace she is not prepared to alter.

"Summersong" by the Decemberists plays.

Sam can't hear the music, but she, like me, appears to have fallen into its rhythm—a steady contemplative walk, taking in what is before her, ears and eyes attentive, even looking upward when the slow roar of a commuter plane climbs in the sky.

Patty Griffin sings "Long Ride Home." And then here's Tom Petty's "Wildflowers" and Steve Earle's "Jericho Road." As we turn south, Sam eyes a cardinal in the parkway grass and follows it, the bird moving to the exact tempo of Paul Simon's "Peace Like a River."

I wonder why I haven't done this before—brought music along on these walks. The songs elevate the steps, as if the walk has a soundtrack, notes meant to enliven the movement. These songs are not motivational gimmicks, not a runner's pulsating playlist meant to stimulate the beats of the heart, but rather a set of melodies for the soul. It is not music designed to pick-me-up or to channel angst—sad songs for a sad day, happy songs for a mood change. It is neither strained nor artificial, but instead unexpected and honest. Psychologists say music can release deep levels of thought and emotion, putting time on hold. And poets, like John Dryden have asked: *What passion cannot music raise and quell?* The answer is somewhere in the genes, I believe, where music is woven into our DNA.

We're home now, and Sam and I walk the driveway to the back entrance of the house. Inside, I unlatch her and call on the living room's smart speaker to connect to my playlist.

George Ezra's "Blame it On Me" fills the room.

"Alexa," I command, "turn up the volume."

Standing before Sam, I slap my hands on my chest. She lifts her paws to me and I take them. The bouncy chords of Ezra's song of love and the consequences of the heart take over the space and Sam and I begin to dance. We sway and we slide, a kind of unabashed two-step. Our movements lack grace, but it does not matter, for the music is all we need, a gift, a little burst of delight, placing a man and his dog in a momentary state of joy.

I hope the young girl at the corner hears her music today, her September playlist. Maybe that's what she had been waiting for, standing there alone on a late summer morning on the edge of autumn.

Walk 28
Night

There are no streetlights lining the roads of our neighborhood. The only lights sit at the top of the tall poles at the intersections. So when Sam and I step out for our walk a couple of hours after sunset, most of the street is black, illuminated only by the entranceway lanterns of silent homes and the television and computer screens glowing through the windows.

It is our first night walk, Sam and I, and Sam is wary.

Leslie and I had eaten a late supper and in the late summer the sun falls fast, so there wasn't much chance of walking in daylight. This is unsettling for Sam. She steps lightly. At the first corner, the sound of a closing garage door—one that would in daylight be virtually unnoticed—rattles her. When headlights from a car toss beams across our backs, she flinches.

"It's okay, girl," I say.

It may seem odd that Sam has not been walked at night. It's simple, really. It's those skunks. When we take Sam out in the backyard before bed to do her business, we keep her on a tight leash away from the tall flowers and bushes along the fence where skunks have been seen toddling by. So, Sam is uneasy about a walk in the dark, like many of us would be about the things we do not know. For me, however, walking tonight is comforting. The musical snap of crickets is in the air; there is a faint smell of wood burning from a backyard fire pit. And beyond the trees in the western sky sits a crescent moon. Beside it is Jupiter, glowing. Mars burns in the south. It's the kind of night sailors thank the gods for; the kind lovers long for.

For Sam, it is menacing.

Sam wears her new leash, a version of the old one, which had frayed from use. It's been a week of new things. Leslie and I celebrated our first wedding anniversary with a stay in Milwaukee to see a small-venue appearance of S. Carey, one of the creative forces behind the band Bon Iver. It was our first overnight stay in Milwaukee. My son Graham is now in his first home. He and his fiancée moved two weeks ago and are settling in. My son Casey is arriving from Seattle in a few days to travel with us to Iowa City, his first trip there, to visit his stepsister, Jen. And here we are, Sam and I, on our first walk together in the dark.

Walking north, Sam stays close, unnerved by the sounds around us. She is startled by the hoot of a night bird, and alarmed by the beep of someone locking their car door.

"I'm sorry, Sam," I whisper.

Night is a beautiful possession; one can own it. The dark is an escape, a silencer of the daylight's disquieting cadence. I think of Thoreau's love of night walks in the woods. I think of the streets of Paris hours after a late coffee at La Palette. I think of the energy of a soft neon-lit walk on MacDougal Street in Greenwich Village or Division Street in Chicago on a weekday evening in winter. And yes, even a walk on a tree-lined suburban street can power down a frenetic day. Night, even now and even here, is a place where one is welcome to hide away.

But that is what it is for me. Not for Sam. For her, this night is Halloween after all the kids in their *Star Wars* costumes have gone home to count their candy and the darkness becomes sinister. Night is Sleepy Hollow. It is Wes Craven. It is Stephen King. It is what H.G. Wells wrote in *War of the Worlds*, the "mother of fear and mystery." Like Sam, I have had gloomy, even scary nights, awful recurring nightmares. And there was the time I was lost after midnight on the streets of London. When I was a kid, I walked through a cemetery after dark on a dare and found myself crying from fear. And there have been times when my soul and heart have been lost in the heaviness of dark days. The evening I had to tell my young children that their mother and I were getting a divorce; the afternoon I held my mother's hand as she took her last breaths in a nursing home bed; the morning the emergency room doctor telephoned to tell me he couldn't save my sister from alcohol.

Sam and I walk slowly near one of the lighted intersections. Rushing through the dark would only worry her. Sam lags just behind on purpose as if remaining one step removed will allow me to protect her. *What would she do without me here?* I wonder. *Would she run to some distant light; would she cower in the bushes?* It occurs to me how much she relies on me, on Leslie. Not only here, but always—to feed her, to brush her, to take her to the vet for the medication that soothes her troubled, itchy ears. When I leave the house alone, she watches me from the window as I walk away. *Where are you going? Will you be back?* And now, she trusts me to guide her through the night. Trusting in and relying on me like those I love—my wife, my children. Even though my sons are grown and on their own, they expect that I will be there, that I will not let them down. It is natural in matters of the heart and in the darkness of our days, for if we cannot trust and rely, we are failing those we love.

At the corner under the lamplight, I ask Sam to sit. I crouch to her level and rub the back of her ears. Her eyes—big and dark—lock on mine. Still, I see in the dim light that they are uneasy, twitching from one side to the other.

"I'm here," I say. Sam licks my hand. "We are almost home. It's just around the bend."

I stand and she does, too. We walk together and again headlights flash across us. Sam stops and turns toward the dual beams. They surely must blind her, creating their own kind of darkness. I touch her head and lead her westward around the corner and down the last block home. High above, just beyond the silhouettes of tall trees, is the moon again, hanging in the sky like a Christmas ornament. It seems bigger, brighter than before. And Jupiter is no longer glowing; it is gleaming. The crickets have traded their disorganized chirp for jazz-like harmony. And as we move closer to home, Sam appears to sense something not easily discernible, a slice of joy, a flash of contentment. She lifts her head to a slight breeze and her pace quickens. This comes not out of fear, I believe, but rather out of gratitude for tonight's companionship. Maybe now, with a small level of faith, she is just a little less frightened of the night.

Walk 29
Jealousy

I'm sitting at the kitchen counter answering previously ignored emails and in between replies and sends, I stand to knock out a few house chores. Dishes left in the sink overnight have been washed and the bed made. I've put away shirts that had been hanging up in the laundry room for days and I'm now tending to a large pile of books once teetering at my bedside. Before leaving for yoga, Leslie had joked that she'd counted thirty-five paperbacks and hardbacks on my nightstand. "Enough to start a little library," she said. This was a not-so-subtle hint. Most of those books are now piled next to me on the counter, soon to be on their way to the writing shed. I'm not prepared to carry them there just yet, and not ready to head to my college office either, as I'm discovering far more overlooked emails. Plus, I'm not dressed for work, sitting here barefoot, unshaven, and wearing old gray gym shorts and a black T-shirt. And Sam is not ready for me to go. She trots toward me with clothing in her mouth— first a brown cotton top and then a beige pullover, both Leslie's, items Sam has snatched from the hamper. *Look what I have. I'm very proud of this.* She then delivers a neon-green tennis ball and nudges it into my lap. *Play with me. Play with me.* She drops the ball at the foot of the stool and steps back to look at me. *Do you see the ball? You must see the ball?* I smile, but mostly I disregard her, feeling a bit guilty about this. Instead, I search my phone for the latest podcast from *The Guardian* featuring Norwegian writer

Karl Ove Knausgård. The battery is at a perilous two percent and I've left my charging cord in the car.

"Damn it," I grumble, rise from the stool, and reach for my keys. "Sorry, Sam," I say.

Sam stands at the entrance to the kitchen and watches me move to the door and outside. *What are you doing? Where are you going? I have the ball right here.*

I lift the cord from my car and as I turn back toward the house's entrance walkway, I see a neighbor, a woman, walking her golden retriever.

"Morning," I say. She says the same, her dog towing on its leash toward me.

"Hey buddy," I say, not remembering the dog's name or the woman's. I rub the top of the dog's head and scratch under its chin.

"She's your best friend, now," the woman says as the dog's eyes widen and its tail wags.

"Oh, you just want a little lovin', huh?" I pat the dog on its back. "Enjoy your day," I say, addressing the neighbor. "You, too, buddy," I add, smiling at the dog. I step toward the front steps, and through the window of the storm door, I see Sam, watching. I wave. Sam only scowls, a piercing glare.

"I'm cheating on you, aren't I, Sam," I joke, reentering the house.

Sam offers no welcoming nuzzle, the kind I have always received when I walk in the door no matter how long I've been gone. There is no wag of the tail. There is no whimper for attention.

"We'll get in a walk, Sam. I promise."

Jealousy is a complicated emotion. Enigmatic. And although veterinarians might insist that dogs do not have dense, complex feelings, what I see before me now is unmistakable jealousy. I wouldn't call myself a jealous person, but I have fallen into its grips, and I know what it is. It has come to me in small bites, nipping at me like an angry Yorkshire terrier or in a big chomp from a German shepherd. Other men have flirted, even in a subtle way, with my wife. I don't like it. I know it is a caveman-like reaction. But it's real. I feel it. I'm not proud of this jealousy. And I wouldn't say I'm insecure, although somewhere deep down, maybe I am. Either way, I try not to show it and most times the jealousy never results in anything of worth; I don't allow it to rule me, trigger me to do stupid things. On this, I am certain. But a dog? I'm not sure how jealousy fully displays itself in Sam, if that's truly what it is.

I put on shoes, toss tap water on my bed-head hair, and snap the leash to Sam's collar. Sam's scowl remains.

The morning is bright, despite a low sun, as autumn is only a couple of days away. We head west past the road construction trucks near the corner. Workers have been building new curbs and will soon repave part of the east-west street. It is not our usual walking route, but I want something fresh today. Sam appears to agree. After a turn south I see a familiar brick home, a Pittsburgh Steelers flag flies at the front door. That's my favorite team, but that's not why I like this home. It's the windows— white, retro, with detailed framing. I like the front entrance with its cozy old-style foyer, more of a mudroom, really. I'd love to have an entranceway like that. Jealous? No, this is envy, jealousy's cousin.

Two houses farther south sits a home with a fenced yard. Sam sees a small red ball on the other side and she pulls toward it. I tug her back and then hear a dog bark and see it show itself at the fence. It is small, brown and white, a mutt. It sees Sam and the barking intensifies. It then seizes the ball in its mouth and runs out of sight. Sam watches, looks at me, and returns to search out the dog. Jealousy? Envy?

Such reviled emotions—painful, hurtful, debilitating. But I wonder if they can be something better if channeled differently. Maybe the emotions can be seen as positive signals of something amiss, something unbalanced, something we can fix, repair. Maybe they are signs of too much emphasis on the material, not enough self-respect, not enough time spent building a relationship or finding a life of contentment. Maybe these emotions are signals, small or big. Maybe experiencing envy leads to curiosity. Maybe when Sam brings me her ball, she just wants me to know the neon-green tennis ball is ratty, dirty, and old, and she wants a new red one.

We cross the street and in the front lawn of another home, sunflowers bloom. Big, bold, and yellow, thriving in the sunshine. They are not wild, but planted on purpose. Someone knows what they are doing. *We have no sun like that in our yard. We can't even grow healthy grass let alone beautiful flowers.*

My bald head wants hair. My sixty-year-old belly wants flatness. I'd like to be taller, but age is shrinking me. Up ahead near the next street, a younger man, maybe in his 30s, marches by on his way to the train station. He's tall, lean, and dressed well in expensive jeans and a dark blue shirt, and he sports a full mane.

"This way, Sam," I say, turning east at the crossroads where I can no longer see him.

On any other morning, jealousy and envy would not have been following me. Most always I can tramp it down when it rises; kill it like a small gardener snake. But there it is anyway, a vermin unearthing itself when Sam sees me with the other dog. It is a small dose. It does not consume me. But the feeling is human. I am human. Sam, she is not. Still, I wonder.

Nietzsche called jealousy and envy the "private parts of the human soul." Therapists have written about how of all the issues of the mind, jealousy and envy are the toughest ones to tame. Malcolm X said that envy blinds us. Socrates called it an "ulcer." Emerson called it ignorance. The Spanish poet, Miguel de Unamuno said "envy is worse than hunger, since it is hunger of the spirit." Emotions like these are festering gashes in our psyche.

But yet, like all other human feelings, it is not the emotion that cripples us, but how we deal with it that debilitates, for those emotions are only chambers in our already fragile hearts.

Sam snivels along a row of red and white impatiens in a garden at the edge of the sidewalk, flowers holding on to what is left of the season. But she is most interested in the mulch and the patches of weeds growing next to the railroad ties the homeowner has used to mark off the garden bed. I wonder what it is she smells. What is so interesting? What's the scent, the aroma? Is it earthy or sweet? Does it smell of the wild? Smell of a rabbit close by? Is it the scent of a squirrel that had once found a nut near the tree? The nose of a dog is an incredible instrument. But I would not want such an intense ability. I do not envy that nose. What I smell as a human is plenty. In the air now is a hint of autumn, like sun-dried leaves. And later, I again will smell the earthiness of coffee or the scent of sea in salmon cooking on a hot iron skillet. Smells I love, smells for me alone. And maybe that is the cure for being strangled by envy, this dubious emotion, to realize it is a destroyer of individuality, of who we truly are by fueling distrust in our own self-worth. Wanting what someone else has taken away from us. We should not accept that. And jealousy, an involuntary emotion born of a past wound, is rooted in our *old* self, someone who no longer is. Still, envy and jealousy live on, rising up unexpectedly to remind us how vulnerable we are.

The east-west street ends at the north-south street and Sam and I choose north. She is done with her sniffing for now, and walks ahead of me. When the leash stretches to its fullest, Sam is tugged backward. She turns to me, as if to wonder why I am not keeping up.

"Hang on, Sam." I say. Sam waits and wags her tail. I stroke her head. "What's the hurry, girl?"

There is none, of course. She is just excited to be here, outside, in the sunshine with me. She knows now that I'm not going anywhere. I'm here with no one else but her, not petting some other dog. I am hers alone.

In a couple of days, Leslie and I will be away from the house for an entire day, some eight hours, renting a truck to move a bed frame, a large rug, and a propane grill from her son's old apartment and hauling everything back home to sell. And during those hours, while Sam is alone, she will stick her nose into my open messenger bag and snatch from it a pair of Bose headphones. She will sit under the table in the living room and chew away, nearly destroying one of the ear pads and leaving teeth marks in the plastic headpiece. I will scold her and Superglue the ear pad back in place. And I will wonder if the destructive behavior came from boredom, if she had been angry that we'd been away so long, or was she jealous that Leslie and I had been together all day long without her.

I will never know the answer, of course. But there are two things I do know: the manifestation of jealousy remains a mysterious thing, and despite the damage, my headphones still work.

Walk 30
Talk to Me

"We simply left you here, all by yourself, didn't we, Sam?"

Leslie and I had returned from a hike at The Morton Arboretum, a 1,700-acre museum of trees a few miles from home. We had walked over three miles through fields of enormous oaks, strands of tall pines, and along trails lined with leafy plants now turning brown in early autumn. And we did it without Sam.

Sam sits under the dining room table, her eyes on me.

"You know we couldn't take you, right?" I ask.

Sam must know I'm apologizing.

"It's the rule," I say. "No dogs allowed. We'd love to take you along if we could."

Leslie works at the dining table, laptop open. She smiles. She knows I do this often, talk like this to Sam. She talks to her, too, but Leslie's words are more of what most dog owners might say—phrases meant to praise, mild discipline, announcements that food and water are waiting. My words, on the other hand, are attempts at conversation.

"We did all that walking this morning," I continue, "but I'm still going to get you out this afternoon. In fact, in just a few minutes, okay?"

Keeping her eyes on me, Sam stands and comes close, her tail gently wagging.

"Yeah, I know. You want to go right this second." I squat before her, and in a high-pitched voice, like a parent talks to a baby, I add, "Don't you worry, I haven't forgotten about you. No, no. I have not. Not you, girl. Not you."

Sam's eyes open wide. I see the whites around her dark pupils. She nuzzles her snout against my right thigh.

"Sam knows what's coming," Leslie says, smiling.

I put away pots and pans that had been left to dry on the rack in the sink, and freshen the water in the small fish bowl, the home of a single guppy purchased a year ago on a whim by my step-daughter and me. I clip the lead, grab a plastic bag, and at the steps to the rear door, as Sam stands in anticipation, I put my nose close to hers and rub my hands on the sides of her head. Again in that high-pitched voice, I ask, "Are you ready, girl?"

I would challenge anyone to prove to me she did not nod with approval.

These conversations are not at all unusual. It would be difficult to count how many times I've encouraged Sam to "hurry up and pee" while standing with her in the frozen backyard in the dark on a frigid February. Or asked, "What do you have now?" when she's dashed through the living room with a stolen article of clothing. Or ordered her to "Stop barking at the old Labrador" that walks past the front window with its owner in the early mornings. I say these things because I believe Sam, at some level, understands. I don't know this for sure, of course. Dog whisperers say that is not the way it works. It takes incredible numbers of repetitive speech for a dog to understand specific words. Highly trained dogs, like police K-9s and dogs used as animals in movies and TV, are continually spoken to in the exact same way, over and over and over. This is not how the typical dog owner communicates. And even with a highly skilled trainer's repetition, dogs will never be able to decipher nuanced sentence structure. But what they can interpret, researchers say, is tone, the highs and lows of speech. Baby talk they get.

Sam's tail is rapidly moving now. She knows I'm about to open the door. And when I say in a squeaky voice, "This is going to be so much fun, girl," Sam balances on her rear legs and reaches her left paw to me, placing it on my lowered shoulder. She knows.

* * *

It is cloudy and cool. I look up to survey the sky.

"You think it's going to rain, Sam?" I ask.

Sam lowers her snout to a small branch that has fallen from one of the big trees in the front of the house. We head south, quickly east, and then north.

"I heard the Cubs beat the Cardinals last night."

Sam looks up at me. She must be aware of how inconsistently the Cubs have played lately.

"I was talking with my students the other day about registering to vote. Do you think dogs should be able to vote? Haven't I asked you this question before?"

Democrat? Republican? Libertarian? Socialist?

Sam spots a small dog at the end of a leash up ahead. It's a tiny one, a little bigger than a Chihuahua. Tan. Scrawny. At the other end of the lead is a tall man, maybe 40 years old, walking as if he is favoring one leg.

"Want to say hi, Sam?"

Sam stands at attention. But when the dog comes close and I ask the man if they can say hello, he does not answer. He stops walking but does not look at me. I allow Sam to nestle up to his dog. But the dog, like the man, has no reaction. No bark. No tail wag. I smile, and the man looks away. "Thanks," I say. He walks on.

"Weird," I say. "It was as if we were not even there."

Sam watches as the man and the dog walk toward the far south corner.

"I guess they don't want to communicate. Not like us, huh?"

Sam turns back to me, we resume the walk, and there are

raindrops.

"Maybe they wanted to get back home before the weather changes."

Sam appears to have already forgotten the awkward exchange and is now inspecting the edge of a lawn for a spot to pee.

"There are some people who have trained their cats to go to the bathroom on the toilet, you know?"

Like the arboretum, the neighborhood is browning. The maples and oaks have not yet turned, but other trees are showing signs of the early season. The real colors should come soon.

"Did I tell you, Sam, it's good to be back in the classroom? The sabbatical was nice. But it is time."

Sam finishes her business and we cross the street. The sidewalk is littered with a few fallen leaves, bronzed with curled edges.

"I always think about my father at this time of year."

Sam is curious about a patch of the parkway that has been cleared of grass, raked and shaped for new sod.

"Dad used to love the fall."

Sam picks up an acorn in her teeth and carries it with us for a few steps.

"We had a dog when I was a kid. It was a big collie. And Dad and I would walk in the woods with her. She was always right by my side. I'm sure we walked at other times of the year. But I only remember the ones in the fall."

Sam drops the acorn and grabs a small stick.

"It's funny how we find ourselves missing people, triggered by something we don't even understand."

The rain is light but steady and we turn at the intersection to head home.

"You probably don't remember your father, Sam. But how about your mother?" Sam has had enough of the found stick and drops it. "Probably not," I continue.

I'm silent for the rest of the walk, enjoying the sound of birds in the distance and autumn's undeniable scent heighted by the drizzle. Still, I can't help thinking of other conversations Sam and I could have—thoughts on the coming winter and whether or not to reseed our lawn before the snow, my calculations for retirement and if it might be possible in a few years, the intense pangs I still feel when I think of my late sister. And what about the world as it is? What would Sam have to say about immigration and women's rights and police brutality? Does she think about global warming and the death of our natural forests? Does she cry about all the junk swimming in our oceans? Does she wonder if angels are real?

At our driveway, I ask Sam to sit. She is puzzled, confused as to why I would ask her to sit here and not on the grass. I have to push her butt down to get her to obey. She stiffens, wary of what might be next. I stroke the hair on her head and ask in a whisper, "Are you happy, Sam?"

Sam tilts her head to the left. Her long lashes flutter.

"I think you are," I say, "but you can't really tell me, can you?" Sam presses her head hard into my hand and I ask again. "Are you a happy, Sam?"

Sam stands, dances around me, then stops and drops her front paws to the ground, arches her back, and raises her tail in the air. She offers a playful snort. I scratch behind her ear and she burrows her head between my knees. Sam cannot talk to me in human terms, of course, but she can listen, and she hears me. I know she does. She hears every single word.

Walk 31
And Now We Rest

Sam stands at the door, watching. From inside the house under the light in the hallway, she studies me as I gather firewood from behind the writing shed and old newspapers from the garage, and arrange them in the fire pit. It takes several matches and some adjustments of the kindling before the fire catches; small sticks ignite first then the bark of one larger log. The glass of the storm door is all that is between Sam and the suburban wilderness of our backyard. Her eyes follow me and then she turns to the flames that are now throwing shaky shadows on the small southwest corner of the lawn. *What could he be doing out there? And why is he doing it without me?* I place the foam camping pad on the hard patio concrete next to the pit and add a second sleeping bag on top for comfort. The bag I will sleep in is made for colder temperatures and I hope it will be sufficient for a night in the low 50s. I stretch it out, kneel to unzip it, and look to Sam, her breath now fogging the door's glass.

There will be no walk tonight. Instead, Sam and I will spend the night together under the twisting clouds of a dark October sky with the moon and the stars giving all they have to shine through. We will rest next to the fire under the magnolia tree in a celebratory sleep, for this is the end of our season of meditative walks. Of course, walking Sam will not end. We will walk together many more times and for years ahead, I hope. But I am back to teaching, the sabbatical is over, and a season—

nearly four months—has passed since Sam and I began what I had hoped would be many contemplative hikes, long and short. What these walks have been will stay with me always. It's been a kind of awakening. But documenting them will be no longer. It is time. Not because I have reached some predetermined number of walks, or that I am weary of the introspection or hyper-observation, or that I am aging, or Sam is aging— although time and its inevitable toll has been a theme through it all—but rather because it is time for these days, these swathes of togetherness to be memories.

I return to the back door to retrieve Sam. Leslie is there to remind me of the skunks.

"I don't want both of you stinking up the place," she laughs.

I assure her that skunks will stay away from our scent and that I once read how they dislike fire. I am making all of this up, but it is a way to allay her fears.

"And you're going to keep the fire going all night?" she asks. "Sparks fly, you know?"

I will not be set ablaze, I insist.

Leslie is not truly worried about these things, I believe, for she knows they are unlikely events. Instead, it is my relative saneness she questions. Leslie is perplexed at why I want to do this when there is a perfectly good bed in the house. But then she catches herself, remembers her days camping years ago, trips out west, and her love of nature. She knows it is the beauty of sleeping in the openness, on the ground, in the breeze of a wilder night, even if wild is only the leafy suburbs. We both know our backyard with its property fence and its two-car garage and its vegetable garden and its lawn furniture is not the Australian outback or the wilds of Oregon. And Sam, well, she is a dog, and what dog does not like the outdoors on an early autumn night?

When Sam and I have taken our walks, we have been like metronomes. Our slow steps have been a countermelody to a world that moves far too fast. When we have stepped off, it has taken time to learn how to remove my foot from the accelerator, to relax my mind, but Sam has shown me the way. She is always only in the moment, and so, I have tried to emulate her pace and with that long-forgotten songs have arrived in my head, lost lyrics have come to me, I have witnessed how the leaves have turned in the breeze; I have noticed the shadows of the sun. Tonight, however, it is not about the walk or the rhythm or the stride or what I am reminded of, it is about the comfort of night and how today's fading sun and the night's rising moon bring the close of a single day, the end of summer, and the end of one chapter in the story of Sam and me.

With Sam on her leash, we walk to our sleeping space. Sam eyes the fire, the outdoor bed, and then me.

"It's just the two of us tonight, girl."

A dog barks in the distance and night birds begin their songs. I always wondered what birds sing at night in the Midwest. Robins? Whip-poor-wills? It's a chatty song—chirp, tweet, chirp—over and over.

"It's not the Rockies or the New Mexico desert, but it's pretty good," I whisper.

My son, Casey has camped at the bottom of the Grand Canyon, bundled up in sub-freezing temperatures. He has slept near glacier lakes and snow-capped mountains. Just a few days ago, he sent me photos of his hike near Mount Baker. His brother has slept on the sandy beaches of Lake Michigan, the woods of Wisconsin and Pennsylvania, and I have slept in the deep forests of the Allegheny Mountains and the bluffs along the Mississippi River. This night is none of these. It is not about comparisons. This night is its own adventure; it carries its own wonder.

I double-up on Sam's lead, locking it to a second one and secure it to a leg of the heavy fire pit. It's not that I'm worried that Sam will run off. The yard is fenced. But there are the skunks.

I stroke Sam's head. "You can stay right here with me." I open the sleeping bag and show Sam the spot where she can rest. "Doesn't that look perfect?"

Sam examines the soft fleece inside the bag, sits, and stretches out her front legs.

From the south, through the trees, I hear the rumble of a train and the bark of another dog. Lights from a passing car flash across the propane grill. The splash of the bright beams startles Sam and she lifts her head and lets out a soft growl.

"It's okay," I say and massage her front paw. There's a rustle in the hosta plants along the fence and Sam growls a second time. "It's okay." *Skunk?* I wonder. I listen and watch. The train moves on, the barking dog quiets, and the fuss along the fence is gone as quickly as it came. I hear only the night birds.

I slip into the bag, fold the pillow in half and rest my head. Sam moves closer and places her head on my right arm. Stretching my left arm across her body, I scratch her back. Light from the fire dances across her face. The smell of wood smoke is all around.

Van Gogh wrote that he often believed that "night was more alive and more richly colored than the day." He shared this in one of his many letters to his brother, Theo. Van Gogh was referring to his work when he wrote this, about how he was sleeping during the day so he could paint at night when the shadings were more vivid. But it would be hard not to believe that the artist wasn't also considering what night does to our higher consciousness, the part of our brain that ruminates over deeper thoughts—the purpose of life, our values, the right way to live. If we accept the night, and especially night in the outdoors, we, like Van Gogh, cannot dismiss its power. Darkness feeds the seeds of rich contemplation. How else could Van Gogh have given us *The Starry Night*?

And so, as the flames of the fire dwindle to embers, and the light in the upstairs window of the house next door is no more, and as Leslie turns off the kitchen lamp before bed, it is the night sky that awakens. Black clouds float across midnight blue. A star flickers and then disappears, and then another does the same. The world softens and I can't help think about the wonder of it all. Not only what I see and hear on this October night, but what the walks with Sam have given me and what they will give me again—time to think, time to feel lonely, time to mourn those I've lost, time to celebrate those I cherish, time to absorb nature, time to wander, time to consider my health and my time left in this universe, time to meditate, time to pray, time to witness the love of a dog. And what have they given Sam? If you believe dogs act only on instinct, then our hikes were about no more than discovering new smells, finding new places to pee, and simple exercise. But I'm not one of those. There must be more. I've seen it on every walk. It is hard to define but it is there. Dog and man, man and dog, in step with each other.

Sam is heavy against me now. Her eyes are closed. I, too, have begun to fade. In short time, I am in a dream, flying above open fields with tall stalks of golden barley below me. On the horizon against the vanishing sun is the silhouette of a gull. How I am able to take flight alongside that bird is of no matter, for it is only an illogical vision that nevertheless is very real. It would be nice to remain here in the dream, rising higher and higher, but instead, I awaken to raindrops—tiny, soft ones on my cheek and forehead. They are no reason to rush to shelter. No reason to dash away. No reason to leave this night and no reason to wake Sam. No reason at all.

Epilogue Walk

It is just dawn when the sun is on a kind of dimmer switch turned to its lowest setting, just enough to pull light into the window but not enough to cast a shadow. My eyes are half-closed, I am awake, and a single sheet of the bedding covers me. Leslie is still sleeping. So is Sam. I am restless.

I'm in love with early morning, always have been. Early before people start to fuss, early before the birds realize they are singing in relative darkness. I am anxious to take in this morning, to walk toward that narrow sliver of the day that is truly its own. So, I stretch and lower my feet to the floor, careful not to disturb Leslie. Sam is in her dog bed next to the wall and she stirs when she sees me. The tags on her collar jingle. Without saying a word, I wave her through the bedroom door to the hallway. I dress in the bathroom, dig for my wool cap and a scarf in the hall closet, and bundle up for cold temperatures. Predictions suggested that it would fall to near freezing overnight. Before bed we placed towels over newly planted mums and snapped off not-yet-ripe late season tomatoes from the garden to save them from frost.

I tuck the book I've been reading, *Wild Comfort*, into the pocket of my fleece vest, thinking I might find a spot along our walk to sit and finish the last two essays. I hook up Sam's leash and head south on the street. Impatiens along the walkway are wilted, acorns crunch under foot, the leaves of two maples at the corner are yellowing.

There is a line in *Wild Comfort* that has been lingering in my head since yesterday when I first read it. This must be partly why I had been restless before rising. "Remember," Kathleen Dean Moore writes, "you are not who you think you are. You are what you do." *You are what you do.* How simple a thought this is. Others have said as much in many ways: Aristotle, Thomas Edison, Ernest Hemingway—philosophers, artists, musicians.

When I started documenting a season of walks with Sam, I had a goal, nebulous in some respects, but there was a relative purpose. At 60, I wanted to rediscover what I believed in, what was important, what I cherished, what I had been and who was I now. My age seemed a good marker, and walking could be a catalyst to understanding. Sam would be there to help me see things fresh. Those walks now are behind me; new walks are beginning.

Sam and I take the street along the tracks and the sun's early rays glint off the silver train zipping by. It is a beautiful sight, really. The train's rhythmic chug drowns out the few singing birds, but it's okay. The clacking is soothing. We walk east along the recently constructed sidewalks but we step on the grass parkway instead. It is still quite green, a contrast with Sam's black hair. When we turn north, the streets come alive. A man stands in his shirt and tie, a leash corralling two dogs. He waits as they pee. A woman in a short black coat hurries to her garage and climbs in her car. I see the reverse lights flash and without looking, she backs up along her driveway, causing Sam and I to quickly stop. And at the corner when we turn west, four men in a red truck park in front of a white brick home and begin to unload an oversized lawnmower, lawn service crews working early. It is a day in a life.

I think of the line in *Wild Comfort* again and realize: *this* is what I do. I see. I hear. I am. I read. I write. I make music on my guitar. I love my wife, I cherish my sons, I adore my dog. I miss my mother's encouraging voice, I miss my father's gift for storytelling, I miss my sister's love of life. I live in the suburb of a big city, but long for the mountains, wilderness, and the sea. I like people; I love solitude. I make coffee. I make a good omelet. I make pretty good chili. I drink whiskey. I drink wine. I play golf but not always well. I treasure friends who are close. I miss the ones who are far from me. I am sometimes lazy. I am sometimes energized. I am hard on myself and sometimes not hard enough. I try to be kind but can be prickly. I try to be fair but often impatient. I walk. I do not run. I hike. I do not rush.

You are what you do.

This is what these walks with Sam have given me, reminders of what it is I do, and in turn have offered reminders of who I am.

When we arrive home, I make coffee and head for the writing shed with Sam next to me. Inside, she rests at my feet. I turn on the space heater, light a candle, adjust the window blind to allow more light to spread across the desk, and I open my journal. With my wool cap on my head and fleece vest wrapped around my shoulders, I begin to write on blank pages what I have come to know.

Acknowledgments

Thank you, Leslie. Thank you, Casey and Graham.

Thanks to all the followers of the original blog series *Walks with Sam*.

Thank you to all the writers of all the dog stories in the world. Each of you knows how special those animals can be.

Thank you to all the Zen masters, meditation and mindfulness teachers who have written and lectured about finding your center and your peace.

Thank you to the nature and the travel writers who have helped me see the world in new ways.

Thank you to the myriad writers, readers, and editors who saw more than what I did in those first weekly blog entries and the first drafts of this manuscript.

Thank you Columbia College Chicago for giving me the time away from the classroom to work on this project.

And thank you, Sam. You are the heart of this book.

About the Author

David W. Berner is the author of several books of memoir and fiction. His work has been honored by the Society of Midland Authors, the Chicago Writers Association, and the Eric Hoffer Book Awards. David has been the writer-in-residence at the Jack Kerouac Project in Orlando, Florida and at the Ernest Hemingway Foundation of Oak Park, Illinois. He lives outside Chicago with his wife and dog.

**ROUNDFIRE
BOOKS**

Put simply, we publish great stories. Whether it's literary or popular, a gentle tale or a pulsating thriller, the connecting theme in all Roundfire fiction titles is that once you pick them up you won't want to put them down.
If you have enjoyed this book, why not tell other readers by posting a review on your preferred book site.

Recent bestsellers from Roundfire are:

The Bookseller's Sonnets
Andi Rosenthal

The Bookseller's Sonnets intertwines three love stories with a tale of religious identity and mystery spanning five hundred years and three countries.

Paperback: 978-1-84694-342-3 ebook: 978-184694-626-4

Birds of the Nile
An Egyptian Adventure

N.E. David

Ex-diplomat Michael Blake wanted a quiet birding trip up the Nile – he wasn't expecting a revolution.

Paperback: 978-1-78279-158-4 ebook: 978-1-78279-157-7

Blood Profit$
The Lithium Conspiracy

J. Victor Tomaszek, James N. Patrick, Sr.

The blood of the many for the profits of the few... *Blood Profit$* will take you into the cigar-smoke-filled room where American policy and laws are really made.

Paperback: 978-1-78279-483-7 ebook: 978-1-78279-277-2

The Burden
A Family Saga

N.E. David

Frank will do anything to keep his mother and father apart. But he's carrying baggage – and it might just weigh him down ...

Paperback: 978-1-78279-936-8 ebook: 978-1-78279-937-5

The Cause
Roderick Vincent
The second American Revolution will be a fire lit from an internal spark.
Paperback: 978-1-78279-763-0 ebook: 978-1-78279-762-3

Don't Drink and Fly
The Story of Bernice O'Hanlon: Part One
Cathie Devitt
Bernice is a witch living in Glasgow. She loses her way in her life and wanders off the beaten track looking for the garden of enlightenment.
Paperback: 978-1-78279-016-7 ebook: 978-1-78279-015-0

Gag
Melissa Unger
One rainy afternoon in a Brooklyn diner, Peter Howland punctures an egg with his fork. Repulsed, Peter pushes the plate away and never eats again.
Paperback: 978-1-78279-564-3 ebook: 978-1-78279-563-6

The Master Yeshua
The Undiscovered Gospel of Joseph
Joyce Luck
Jesus is not who you think he is. The year is 75 CE. Joseph ben Jude is frail and ailing, but he has a prophecy to fulfil …
Paperback: 978-1-78279-974-0 ebook: 978-1-78279-975-7

On the Far Side, There's a Boy
Paula Coston
Martine Haslett, a thirty-something 1980s woman, plays hard on the fringes of the London drag club scene until one night which prompts her to sign up to a charity. She writes to a young Sri Lankan boy, with consequences far and long.
Paperback: 978-1-78279-574-2 ebook: 978-1-78279-573-5

Tuareg
Alberto Vazquez-Figueroa
With over 5 million copies sold worldwide, *Tuareg* is a classic adventure story from best-selling author Alberto Vazquez-Figueroa, about honour, revenge and a clash of cultures.
Paperback: 978-1-84694-192-4

Readers of ebooks can buy or view any of these bestsellers by clicking on the live link in the title. Most titles are published in paperback and as an ebook. Paperbacks are available in traditional bookshops. Both print and ebook formats are available online.

Find more titles and sign up to our readers' newsletter at
http://www.johnhuntpublishing.com/fiction

Follow us on Facebook at https://www.facebook.com/JHPfiction
and Twitter at https://twitter.com/JHPFiction